THE UBER-GROOVER

THE UBER-GROOVER

(UNEDITED, UNFORMATTED, DOCUMENTED)

TAKE THE RIDE OF YOUR LIFE, WITH THE UBER-GROOVER!

A NOVEL BY

M. J. MANLEY

Strategic Book Publishing and Rights Co.

Strategic Book Publishing and Rights Co., LLC
USA | Singapore
www.sbpra.com

For information about special discounts for bulk purchases please contact Strategic Book Publishing and Rights Co. Special Sales at bookorder@sbpra.net.

ISBN: 978-1-68181-663-0

Prelog:

After fifteen-years of rehabilitation, a veteran, injured during the war; takes on a whole new mission: Driving as an UBER- GROOVER!

The UBER-GROOVER LYRICS: WizKhalifa & Curren$y- UBER DRIVER 1.

Briskly, but then again, the morning was Sultry, with the dew and mist collaborating with the fog of the Pacific Ocean near the Santa Monica Pier. The day was not unusual than any other day at The Veterans Hospital. People were transporting themselves to work that morning on the Interstate 405 freeway, while the truck drivers throttled in full gears to make their deliveries, the morning of April 15, 2016. You can smell the bacon and sausage cooking in the kitchen as the workers, dressed in all white, flipped over the hot cakes and battered up the home made biscuits. Nurses, were filing into the hallways, getting their assignment, while the doctors and the technicians stood in line at the Starbucks to get their daily dose of coffee. For the past fifteen years, at the Veterans Medical Center, in West Los Angeles, California; it was routine; an everyday event and nothing at all unusual for Mitchell to have observed for that morning.

"Mitchell Martinez" said the orderly.

"Yeah-that's me" as I responded, sitting up from my bunk and straightening up my legs, swinging them to the right while I rolled up my sleeves to have a needle placed in my arm too get a blood sample that morning; just as I did every other morning while a patient at The Veterans Medical Center.

"Your blood will be drawn before you leave Mr. Mitchell"

"Leave, when am I going to be leave Dorothy" I asked the orderly, who has been my assistant nurse for the past fifteen years, while I went through multiple surgeries, rehabilitation and therapy from battle scares suffered from the war.

"It says here in your chart, that you will be checking out today and going to your orientation for your new job placement"

"Really, I mean; everything was approved-the license, the background check and did they modify a vehicle for me to drive" I was elated, that after all those years of being a patient and a outpatient at The Veterans Hospital, I will finally be independent and on my own, driving a vehicle for a transportation company.

"Congratulations Mr. Martinez and good luck with your new job"

"Thank you Dorothy-Well, Dorothy, can you tell me, this time, will things work out better than the last times that I tried to work, independently"

"It will work out for you, that is, if you want it too work for you-just take one day at a time and if you need help, just call one of your counselors or come into the hospital and they will be glad to help you along in your new career"

"Career, well how can I be getting a new career at the age of fifty. I have been through three wars and my body is beat up with pins and titanium screws all the way from my toe to my neck-what kind of career will I have as a driver at this age in my life"?

"Uber"

"What was that nurse Dorothy", as I thought she had hiccupped or made a sly remark as she sometimes did, being that she has been my assistant nurse for the passed fifteen years as I underwent surgeries and therapy for war time wounds.

"That's what it says here, you will be driving your new car for Uber, you will be trained to be a Uber Driver and they have furnished you with a brand new Chevrolet, especially modified car; you see here; this is the picture and all the things you got to know and will learn as a driver"

"Who will I drive"?

"People-that want to go places"

"You mean, like a taxi driver" I asked Dorothy.

"Oh no, my daughter takes Uber all the time; to the movies, to the market, it is a inexpensive transport system that people use from all walks of life Mitchell"

"Oh yeah-well, why did they choice me; I drove gas tankers in the Army; that is, before they placed a bomb in the road and blew the whole tanker and me too pieces-I have not never driven no people Dorothy"

"There is a first time for everything-I think you will do well driving people-you're a people's person and you always helped the other veterans over the years with their disabilities"

"Will they pay me to drive"?

"Oh yes, I heard that they pay pretty good-here, this is the package, right here in this box-all of the instructions and you can go to the library and put the disc into the computer and you can start your training lessons"

"That's a big box, what else does it have inside of that box"

"Here, this is a cell phone, emergency kit; your Wi-Fi, XM, radio, blue tube instructions…and contact kits, and yellow and orange jacket for on the road emergencies"

"Oh no, I am not doing that; it's a trap for me too drive for the military again-I am not getting blown up again Dorothy-can't you see what they are trying to do-they are putting me into the Danger Zone, so I can get the rest of my body torn too threads so they can stop giving me that pension check"

"No they 'ain't' Mr. Martinez, you need to go and see that Psychiatrist before you leave this here hospital; you are having those delusions again"

"Delusions-you give me a box of things that says UBER, and tell me that I am having Delusions; what the hell is a UBER anyway"

"Just get ready to check out Mr. Martinez, your trainer will tell you everything that you need too know-why you should be thankful that President Obama is trying to do something for you Veterans-get you all back on your feet again"

"Back on my feet-why these plastic toes and angles-you call that back on my feet-you mean back on Mr. Johnson and Johnsons feet, why they are the ones that made these prosthetic feet-these 'ain't' my feet Mrs. Dorothy; these are phony feet, just like that UBER Box with all that equipment-I don't know how to use a cell phone and how am I going to press those little buttons on that thing with these steal fingers"

"Mr. Martinez, now you are the one that told the doctors and the counselors that you wanted to drive again-now come on, get ready for your training-look Mr. Martinez, what would you rather do, stay here at the hospital, with all the rest of these amputee's and watch the pigeons and the 405 freeway traffic the rest of your life"

"Watch the pigeons-I am the pigeon, why they are using me for another one of their experiments-Uber, I never heard of that before"

"You never heard of it because you have not been out of here for the past twenty or more years-now get your things together and dress nice for your Uber Training session-it may lead to something better"

"Alright, already, I will see what happens, now hand me my legs and my arm and I will go to the library and watch the Uber training disc-maybe, there may be a chance for this to work for me"

"Well, there are lots of veterans that drive for the company and you will fit in well, since you like to help people"

"Veterans, the young ones, like I was, when I came here some fifteen years ago-without legs and one arm-now, they got all of this electronic stuff that they can tell the Fingers what to do and they will do that for me; Said Martinez.

"Well can you tell those legs over there to walk over here so I can put them on you and that arm so you can eat your breakfast and be ready to go to your UBER training session"

"What do I do after the training, where do I go Dorothy"

"Here, it says you will be going to a special rehabilitation center in Long Beach-there, they have given you a place with a kitchen and you will have Independent Living Quarters"

"Well that is just great and just to think, it took them almost thirty years to get me back on my feet"

"You mean Johnson and Johnson feet"

"Oh, your funny Mrs. Dorothy; but I will miss you, you and all the rest of the team that helped me throughout the years"

"We will miss you too Mr. Martinez, now, get ready, they will be here to pick you up and take you too the motor pool where you will get your brand new car with all the modifications for you to drive for your new job"

"Okay-I will give this UBER thing a try-thank you and I will let you know how things work out Mrs. Dorothy"

Chapter I

Training Day One

Building 258, of the Brentwood Barracks, were once a facility used for the military reserves during a time of war and now used as dorms for the veterans that "Bored The Battles of War" quarters where rehabilitation and training takes place for those veterans injured fighting for freedom. A land Grant, given to The United States Federal Government by the Spaniards with The Four Quarters of Wilshire Boulevard as The Medical Center lies overlooking the 405 freeway on the South West side, while directly across The 405 Interstate Freeway, The United States Federal Building lies on the South East side that in houses the Federal Bureau of Investigation; The Immigration and Naturalization Department and the Department of Veterans Affairs Office (V.A.) administrative office in The Tower.

The lone, tranquil place where the last standing grounds for the Veterans lie on the North East side, The Veterans National Cemetery where the Veterans that served their country lie in peace. The four corners of The Spaniard Land Grant, given to The Veterans of the United States in 1889, now worth billions of dollars but can not be sold as a commercial acquisition or leased out. Prime property, since Bel Air is adjacent to the University of California Los Angeles, lies in the North East of the Quad of Brentwood, Beverly Hills, the homes of the rich and the famous lie in the same area where the price tag is "Priceless".

"Martinez, Mr. Mitchell Martinez" a bearded man wearing a dungy gray pants with matching shirt called out my name as I sat in the wheel chair in the hallway waiting to see what they have for me; training as a transportation driver for a company called UBER.

"That's me," I answered, as I grabbed my brown bag with my belongings as the escort released the brakes of the wheel chair and began to role me outside toward the downward ramp where my home has been for the past decade and a half.

"My name is Larry and I am your representative and trainer for your driving job," said this Larry, as I glanced at his stenciled name and to whom he works for. It said: Motor Pool.

"What is this Uber thing Larry and why was I chosen to drive"

"Transportation was your MOS, so we have placed you in the Independent Living Training program to get back on you're your feet; well, sort of to speak" As Larry looked down at the foot rest, he had to catch himself since my legs were gone and just prosthetic plastic joints and fillers are under my pants. It happens all the time with people once they see that enormity of having no legs but the one's that the V A specially built for me that resembles the actual legs that I lost in the war.

"Oh, I am sorry," said Larry.

"Oh, I am use to it-now tell me Larry, are you going to be my trainer and will this new car be my car"

"Yes Mr. Martinez; from the compliments of the Department of Vocational Rehabilitation-the car, which is a brand new Chevrolet Malibu, four door six cylinder is all your whether you like your new job or not"

"Really, so what is the catch-I mean, if it is too good to be true, chances are, it is not true" I told Larry, as he continued to wheel me to a chaffered van that had a hydraulic lift that raised up and placed me inside the van truck.

"I will show you how to use your new cell phone that directs you straight to your passenger that you will pick up and take to their designated place"

"Designated place, and where may that be"

"It is right on the cell phone, all that you must do is listen to the voice command and you will be lead directly to your passenger by satellite Google"

"Do you mean to tell me that the vehicle will drive itself"?

"Just about, but you must remain in the vehicle since that is the State of California Law, a person must be present; although you do have some control of the vehicle"

"You got to be pulling my leg" I laughed and said archaically, knowing, I only have prosthetic legs and Larry had a since of humor and we both laughed at the whole idea that Google, The Department of Transportation; the Vocational Rehabilitation Department, has received billions of dollars to devise a vehicle, that pick up passengers, driven by satellite called: UBER.

Strapping me down in the van; I could see through the window Mrs. Dorothy Chavez and the other orderlies that helped me and all the other veterans that were injured; help us veterans get our life's back together after we gave it our best and went in their and got the job done at the risk of our salvation to survive with our bodies breaking up.

"This is the Chevy, all automated and all designed just for you to: Pick Up, Stay In Vehicle, and Drop them off all on the designated drop off point right on the cell phone"

"Wow, it sure has been modified-the throttle or accelerator is on the steering wheel and the brake is a peddle on the right side of the steering column-Black, with tinted windows-it looks like a Mobsters Car"

"No, it's a UBER/Google Transportation Vehicle and it is yours"

"Can I sit in it"?

"Why, sure; get use to it-now it has Blue-Tube, so you can receive calls and hear the calls from the speaker systems, it has WI-FI, that you can receive designated points of pick ups and drop offs that feeds right from the satellite that will automatically guide your vehicle to pick up and drop off"

"All these years has past and I am in the dark of all this new technology; I thought to myself."

"It will take a few days for you to get use to but according to your aptitude test, you are very intelligent and able to solve problems quickly"

"Oh, that's why they choose me-from those test I took a few months ago-I knew it was some reason why they choose me from all the other Paraplegics and Disabled Veterans"

"That was just one of the criterions-there were several more that made you one of the top persons for the new UBER? GOOGLE Trans."

"Okay, let's get started" I was excited; here I am in the year 2016, a totally disabled veterans being used for this secret experimental transportation mode of driving. It has already build up my self esteem and gave me something to look forward to after spending day after day, month after month as a patient and out patient at The Veterans Hospital. I breathe a sign of relief as I was given Hands on Driving Experience and the new Cell Phone Technology-It Is A Miracle!

If you can name it, the UBER CAR Has It. Fax machine in the back seat pulled out from the passenger seat. Satellite Radio that can receive any station, world wide, even television stations right on the radio and all I had to do is use the screen of my new cell phone to watch a movie while the radio carries the sound-there was a second delay between the sound and the actual picture but it worked for me. Emergency backup button and On Star technology for the back up driving routes just in case the Google Directions Failed. The Chevy Malibu, UBER/GOOGLE Transportation Vehicle is a Geriatric James Bond Movie Dream Come True.

"Now, for your first trip to your Independent Living Residence"

"You think I am ready"

"Yes, you are more than ready after two weeks of training, you did very well on your On Site Driving test and now, the Big One, from West Los Angeles to Long Beach, California driving your UBER/GOOGLE Transport Vehicle"

"Oh no, I am not getting on the 405, freeway; it will be a disaster just waiting to happen"

"Don't worry, we will be following you with our Drone System and Satellite System with your every move Mitch"

"Two, three in the morning-I know your don't plan on sending me to Long Beach on a busy morning commute traffic hour Larry"

"That is exactly what we are going to do-at three o'clock, this afternoon, on this day, Tuesday, May 24, 2016, your first solo run Mitch Martinez"

"They spent billions of dollars on this technology and I will be the Pilot to this project-what a opportunity-I always wanted to be successful in the military and I got rank real fast, that is, until I was caught up in a IUD bomb right outside of Afghanistan. My entire world collided when that day just took my spirit and my very soul from me. One Bomb, several lives wasted and maimed beyond repair but now that I have a chance to prove myself, why not use up this opportunity for my best interest.

Feeling like a jet pilot at the realm of a new Stealth Bomber-I pressed the start button and received a cue on the voice monitor that the brake system is okay, the steering system, the transmission system, the electrical system; all systems including the data system were on cue. Now all that was required from me is to say: GO. The go pro monitors were adjusted in the rear and on the front windshield to my height and gave me all angles of me and the possible passengers that were to board the new, innovative transportation system.

From the motor pool hanger, the doors opened and the ray of light entered the storage area beaming in through the front windshield of the Modified Chevy.

"All systems Go" I was in the driving seat as I adjusted my self and prepared for the ride of a lifetime. Through the Brentwood Veterans Rehabilitation Hanger, the speed remained steady as the vehicle satellite system kicked in and notified me of a stop in fifty feet. The vehicle paused for ten seconds and once being a driver of heavy duty vehicles, I did take the liberty of looking both ways as the Chevy proceeded, all on it's own; driving itself, as if there was a person at the wheel. For a matter of fact, the dashboard indicated all the vehicles, the buildings, and the people that were on the streets walking in full

3-deminsional color.

"Wow"

"Is there a problem Mr. Martinez"?

"Oh no-it's just that, this car is really doing what it has been programmed to do-it is driving itself"

"Well, congratulations- your mission is being accomplished and you are on board of a historical adventure"

"Yes, this is amazing Larry-it is as if I am watching a movie on three dimensional holographic vision and the sensors are monitoring everything"

"Everything is going according to plan Mr. Martinez"

"Thank you"

"What was that Mr. M."?

"Thank you for letting me be part of this project"

"Thank you for accepting the mission of being the first UBER/GOOGLE Unmanned Driver of a transportation vehicle: U.G.U.D.T.V.

"Amazing" that was all that I could say, as the vehicle, without any of my controlling the steering wheel, shifted to the right to enter The Fabulous 405 Freeway"

"Now comes the challenging part," I thought to myself, since the 405 freeways is regarded as one of the busiest freeways in the entire world and it was RUSH HOUR!

"It ready the traffic condition" As I reported, from my training with the vehicle, the data read out heavy traffic conditions and a accident one quarter mile in lane one of the 405 freeway.

"Larry, will it direct me to a alternate route"?

"No, it will resolve the situation itself, just relax and enjoy the view"

"The voice monitors are recalculating the time of my arrival Larry but not to my apartment in Long Beach; it is giving me a Pick Up, at Palms near Olympic and Sepulveda"

"Well now, you got your first pick up-let your Google map induct you Mr. M to your destination and set your criterions for the pick up"

"Okay Larry, or shall I call you Mr. L"

"Larry will be just fine" This was beginning to be like a science fiction movie-who would ever though that I would be at the Helm of a automatic vehicle guided to control it's own destination and pick up times.

"Larry, Larry Shultz, how do I know who I am picking up; will the persons picture pop up on the screen"? I had to ask, since I could be picking up anybody at any time. That is one question that I did not ask during the two weeks of training.

"Uber/Google, screens all of their riders; they get their driver license and identity, so you need not worry Mitch; if any thing happens we will track the person down and see to it that they are prosecuted and they will never ever be able to ride a UBER/Google car again" Larry Shultz explained to me but there was one little thing that he did not mention: HOW ABOUT ME, WHAT WILL HAPPEN IF I AM ATTACKED LIKE THE OLDER SYSTEM UBER DRIVER LAST YEAR THAT WAS BEAT UP BY A TACO BELL EXECUTIVE? Oh well, it was all in the mission and I was adamant in getting this first rider done and completed. With the Billion Dollars spent on all this High technology; people's personality was not in the equation.

"Your destination will be on the right hand side 500 feet away," said the Google Map.

"Okay" I responded, naturally; knowing that the Lady inside the machine will not respond back; but she was like my Seeing Eye Dog and the only communications, besides Larry at the UBER/Google headquarters that I could rely on.

"You have reached your destination," she said.

"Thank you" I responded.

"Placing my U, UBER sign in on the front windshield, that will identify me as a UBER Driver and the patron will see that I am there to pick them up and take them to their destination, safely and professionally. Rolling down the electric window.

"Sir, did you order a Uber Driver" I said, looking out the window and I was startled-it was Larry and his assistant Carl Smith, already opening the back door of my UBER vehicle and getting inside, congratulating me on my first successful trip with The Newly High Technical UBER/Google Mobile.

"Congratulations Mr. Mitchell Martinez on your first trip outside the UBER Center and now, Carl and I will present you with this Plaque as an Official UBER/Google driver" I was stunt, knowing that I was the first UBER/ Google driver too test this new, innovative system that The United States Government, along with UBER and GOOGLE has Launched for the Disabled Veterans who suffered debilitating injuries and psychological impairments during the wars and now we will be given another chance in life; a new mission. Not so unusual than the last mission of protecting the freedom and democracy of the citizens; for I will be still making certain that the people are served with adequate transportation to and from their workplace, the airports, the markets where they live and to their church where they pray and to the schools where they learn more about themselves and the world.

All in all, that was the reason that I enlisted into the Army; to serve and too protect, so, once again, I will be serving the citizens in my own neighborhoods by driving them to their destinations, safely and courteously.

"Why, thank you Larry, Carl; this award is for me" I asked, almost shedding tears of joy.

"It sure is; you see Mitch; you are the first UBER/GOOGLE driver that was trained successfully to carry on the mission to drive people with all the new technology and it will get bigger and better" said Larry.

"We recorded and copied the entire process and now we are off to Washington, D.C., to present this new innovative transportation idea and process to The President of the United States and to Congress" Carl interjected his assignment of being the assistant in the whole process of getting me ready and prepared to drive the new technological advanced mode of transportation.

"Now, we are off to the airport, so set your Google function on START NAVIGATION and let leave the driving to UBER Mitch"

"Will do Larry, Carl-but, but, what will I do when you are gone; who will give me directions, who can I call while you two are out selling this new technology and training other Veterans and young college students that want new jobs in the transportation field" I asked and got a little shaken up, since, for the past two weeks, Larry and Carl, saw to it that I woke up with the cell phone in my hand and pressed the appropriate buttons to get "Online" with UBER in a Drive Simulator at the main headquarters in Santa Monica near the Veterans Hospital. What will I do now?

"Just let UBER be your guide; it will tell you everything you want to know Mitch; how to get started, where to pick up and drop off" said Larry.

"All that you got to do is press that "U" button on your cell phone, and it will go directly to the satellite hundreds of miles in the sky, that will bounce off to the headquarters and hit The GOOGLE Application, that will bounce back to your UBER CAR, and turn on all the systems and target in your destination and all that you got to do is put on your gear and go out and pick up, and drop off" said Carl.

"What if, I mean, the passenger, what if they see that I have no legs and I only have one good arm Larry, Carl; they may laugh at me and they may take advantage of me and steal my UBER Car and leave me on the streets" I had to asked them that question.

"We thought that you would inquire into that; you see Mr. Martinez, this process of letting the Veterans did not just happen over night; we screened the college students, we screened the prisoners and we screened even the undocumented workers and from all the applicants that we screened to take over the task of driving in this new Billion Dollar System, The War Veterans, with their prior training, came out on top and you are the first prototype Mitch" Wow, I thought to myself, me, the first and now they are taking this demo, of me to Washington, D.C. to address the congress and the President about receiving more funding and training for the Veterans-I will succeed in my new mission without prejudice....

"You will reach your destination in 1000 feet," said the cell phone Google Application.

"But Larry, what will happen if I got to get out of the vehicle to unload their luggage-without legs, it will be hard to do"

"You have legs, the federal government bought them for you and they are attached to sensors and you see that red beam on the front of the rear view mirror, it notifies The Bell Hops, at the airport that assistance in needed to unload luggage for the passenger at American Airline; Southwest Airlines; Delta Airline and, well, look at the list in your glove box and it will tell you all about all the Airlines that participate in the UBER Movers Projects"

"The UBER Mover Project-wow Larry, you have a name for everything don't you-I guess you will be calling me: The UBER GROOVER, since I have not been out of the V A yard since The Eighties & Nineties" I joked with Larry and Carl before the two had the Airport Hops unload their luggage to board a plane to Washington, D.C., to talk to Congress and maybe the entire world about the new mode of Transportation: The UBER MOVERS System.

Chapter II

The UBER Apprentice

ou have reached your destination; your destination is on the right. As the Google map voice notified me. My Girl Gina, that's what I named her; from an old girlfriend that I had in High School. We occasionally wrote each other and then, she faded out, after I was medevac to Germany after the IUD injury that changed my life. I would not have to worry about my new Gina though. She can be turned off and turned on with my voice control and she is always in my corner, as I turn the corners and by ways with her (Gina) giving me the right directions in my new life.

"Self Storage Facility at La Ciendaga and Slauson -G-Girl" as I gave G, for Google, Gina the call for my destination in order for me to stop, briefly at my Storage facility that I have kept for years; storing my cloths and old family pictures. I have pictures before entering the military with all of my extremities. My prostetic leg were strong as steal; probably not as strong as these steal, titanium one's issued and electronically programmed by Johnson and Johnson researchers, but, I ran track with my God Given Legs and was the fastest 100 meter runner in California. This government issued legs would not have had a chance on the dusty track field. The sensors in the calves would accumulate too much dust and cram up. My old legs that were cut off and demolished were my best legs; now, I have two nobs, left and right, that irritates me if I stand on them too long.

"Mr. Martinez, how long has it been" said Markus; the office manager, to who I had not seen for many years, but the storage has been paid for by direct debuts from my disability pension check for the last ten or more years.

"Your still working here" I was surprised as Marcus was; for he was here when I had the movers bring my cloths and other items that were shipped from the Hospital in Germany years ago; where I had my legs amputated and later moved to The Veterans (Four Corners) Medical Facility in West Los Angeles, California. He looked, inside the Malibu Uber car; as I surmised that he was looking, not at the car but too see, how and the hell I was driving the vehicle. I had not received my new legs the last time that I visited the Storage facility.

"Doing better now Marcus"

"Well, I can see that-is that a new car your driving"

"Twenty-Sixteen, especially equipped for me Markus"

"Wow, it sure is a nice looking mobile; do you remember your gate code to get inside to your storage Mr. Martinez"

"No"

"Well, it's been so long, those old codes wouldn't have worked anyway-here, let me let you inside and I will reprogram the new code and write it down for you-now you can change it to the password that you can remember once you receive the code Mr. Martinez"

"Can you send it to this email; I can automatically recode it once I receive it on my Computer right here in my car"

"What's all those gadgets and monitors you got inside their and that bubble, that thing on the top of the roof, what the hell is that; you doing emergency rescues Mr. M"

"No, that's the new Signal source that guides the car and communicates with the road and the other cars"

"You mean to tell me-this is one of those cars that drive themselves"

"Yes, this is a UBER/Google mobile"

"Why I be, my oh my, this technology has blown the roof off of everything that was in the past-you mean to tell me that you ain't got to steer or press the gas peddle"

"I could not do it even if I tried with these steal legs Markus"

"You say, you got some new legs"

"Yes, but there has got to be someone always inside the car; California Law"

"Okay Mr. Martinez, you are all set; I got the gate open and now you can tell your, what you call it: UBER/Goo"

"No, it's a car developed by UBER and GOOGLE too transport people too work, too school and to the Airport, automatically; by satellite controlled by computers"

"What, well, I am done with all of this techno…whatever you say; so, so, I might as well pack up my things, right now; those computers will soon take over my job"

"It will be a while Mr. M. Moore before your job is at risk-security and the human element will always be needed to protect the people's most cherished items"

"Yeah, you got a point there-only got a few more years before retiring, you got a point-well, stop by sometimes and tell me more about that You Bert GOO thing that you are driving now, I mean, that is driving you Mr. M."

Okay-Storage number A-50 G" I made the command and the car automatically moved throughout the storage facility slowing down at each and every door of the facility as if it was viewing what was inside of the doors that people have stored their personal items. Like a x-ray machine, Google found my storage. I had almost forgotten myself where my small storage was and then, Gina (The Google-Gal) stopped.

"This is it, and I guess, I will have to temporarily shut you down G-Girl and put my legs on and open the door to my storage and grab a few cloths"

"You have reached your requested destination"

"Thank you-G"

"Your Welcomed"

"What-why that was not in the program-G-Girl can feel me out and she is adding language to it's memory and voice recalls, amazing, scary, but incredible" It took me a whole half an hour to place my legs in the right socket and walk over to the door-there was my old High School Locker Combination Lock-now, if I can just remember the number: 39-11-29; that's it, Walla, it opened-now; there they are, marked on the box, my cloths; sweaters, jackets and shoes; a little hat that my grandmother made me to keep my head warm when I was stationed in Germany; God Bless Your Soul-I got to go and visit her grave site one day-her spirit won't recognize me without a arm and steal legs; oh well, I won't recognize her either-she's been gone for many years but what she taught me about people will last forever-always be polite because you never know when you are going to need that person-I will never forget what she instilled in me.

Box one, box two and one more, inside the truck of my UBER/G; that is all that will fit-now, let me close the door, and; wow, here are a box of pictures, the old me-I do not want to see these pictures right now-it will throw me off my game-I am doing good for once in my life and do not need no psychological trauma, right now in my life-let me snap off these legs and be on my way-better yet, I will keep the legs on and maybe, on my way to my home in Long Beach, I will pick up a passenger, a real passenger. My apprenticeship training is over, now it is time to get to work.

"G-Girl, let's roll"

"Your Command is Clear, Proceeding to Slauson and La Ciendiga, Inglewood, California main route, Long Beach, California, Residential Care Facility, Del Amo Boulevard and Cherry Street, proceeding Mr. M"

Chapter III

Clients that Care!

"Beep, beep, beep…Mr. M, client in Hawthorne, California at 11456 Hawthorne Boulevard, destination; Torrance Memorial Hospital, shall I proceed"

"Roger on that G-Girl, let's test the waters and proceed when ready" Wow, this will be my first client, besides Larry and Carl; let me straighten out my legs and adjust my prosthetic arm, pulling down the sleeve so the client will not be scared of the steal fingers and plastic coated arm-the G-Girl, took the easies route, right down Sepulveda avenue making a left turn on El Segundo, then right on Hawthorn Boulevard.

"Your destination will be reached in 1000 feet…. you have reached your destination…." Said G. that must be her right there; she looks like she is waiting for a UBER ride…

"UBER Maim" I rolled down the electric window and my UBER-U sign was visible-she opened the door and slide her self on the back seat and closed the door.

"How are you maim"

"Just fine-I have a doctors appointment at Torrance Memorial today"

"Why sure Maim, I will take the most convenient route and have you there in the designated time-do you have enough leg room and there is water in the pocket of the back seat"

"Why thank you, why this is a nice UBER car"

"Yes maim, it is the top of the line, new, automatically controlled vehicle and you are officially the first UBER Automatic Mobile Passenger Rider"

"Oh, really-I love UBER, it is so convenient and inexpensive, why if I would have taken a Cab, it would have cost me Sixty or more dollars just to go to my doctors appointment" said Mary, I got her name from my Google Map, cell phone, right at the bottom and I could, by pressing a application on the phone, find out all the information about Mary-it would not be necessary, since Mary, with a Philippine accent, I knew she was no threat and all my sensors on my monitor x-rays application did not detect any knives, guns and even a hair pin inside Mary's purse-she passed the automatic screening test and we proceeded to take her to her programmed destination.

"If you do not mind me asking, what happened to your arm"?

"Oh, I do not mind-I was in the war and my truck was bombed by a IUD, that is an explosive bomb and I lost my arm and legs"

"Oh, I am so sorry; thank you, for serving us in the military, my husband retired from the Navy; he was stationed at Cebu Bay, in the Philippines but he lost his life a few years ago from cancer"

"Oh, I am sorry to here that Maim-now you receive his benefits"

"His benefits, what benefits"

"Well, if you were married to him maim, you receive benefits from his pension"

"No, you see, we were married but he moved back to the Philippine and I went there to go bury him and I never received any thing from the Navy"

"Maim, you are entitled too his pension, since you were still legally married-take down this number and call: 800-827-1000 and the counselor will explain thing too you on your eligibility"

"Oh really, oh, here we are"

"You have reached your destination," said G-Girl, my Google Guide.

"Oh, thank you very much, I will call the number you gave me as soon as I get home and thank you for your service"

"Thank you Mary and have a nice day" Wow, the first passenger and after being in the system of the Veterans Hospital, I gave her some advise that may get her some benefits-this UBER thing is working out pretty good, for I always wanted to help serve the people, the good people and that is why I enlisted into The Army. Now that I am a civilian, I can still help, I can still drive and I can go to my outpatient appointments. It all came together, in my life, at this very moment.

"Beep…beep…beep…client at: Westin Hotel, Long Beach Marina at: 123 Ocean Boulevard, destination; Long Beach Municipal Airport…

"I accept the mission…let's roll G"

"You will reach your destination at 11:47 a.m. to pick up two clients and arrive at the Long Beach Airport at: 12:35 p.m., Jet Blue airlines-the route with the least traffic has been programmed on your Google Drive Mr. M."

"Roger, let's role G-Girl" We were out, for the second client of the day; a two passenger pick up, so they will be prorated for more money with two people-this is getting good. Oh, this is the amount of money from my last client; wow, only $8.76 cent; that pretty cheap for a twelve mile drive all the way from Hawthorn to Torrance-that's why Mary, the client, said she loves using UBER, for eight dollars she could not beat that price and she gave me five stars, why that is a feather in my cap; that is a perfect score and I will get a good evaluation with five stars. I hope that she did not give me those five stars feeling sorry for me-I did not want her to even see my arm but these sleeves must have moved up and she noticed. I do not want people to feel sorry for me-I am doing what I want and driving is what I want to do.

"Warning, heat sensor on right leg indicating a sudden rise in temperature" said G-Girl…

"Oh, I accidently pressed the seat warmer that went too my leg sensor and over heated my wires inside my prosthetic leg-let me turn off the heat and turn on the air and I will have to report this incident…

"All is well, G-Girl" I responded and reported the incident…

Knowing the Federal Government, the Department of Vocational Rehabilitation and now, The UBER/GOOGLE Partnership, they going to want something out of this. Not just knowing that, from my talents, skills and using me as a so called "Guinea Pig" so other IUD inflicted veterans can get "Gainful Employment" Congress, The United States Senate and The Department of Defense wants results to bring down the deficit.

Twelve trillion dollars in deficits is a lot of dough, I thought to myself, so, if they can prove to take at least five billion dollars a year employee veterans in this new concept of UBER/Google, well, there you go; government wins, veterans lose, once again. Maybe I should not think like that, but that is the way of the world, cost down and there is no such thing as a free lunch.

"Beep, beep, beep…" I got the signal, there is another mission to be ran; let me accept the challenge.

"Your destination is Wilmington and Imperial Avenue; make a U-Turn on Wardlow and proceed to the 710 freeway" said the Google G-Girl; as the Google automatic directions were programmed through the vehicle and all I had to do is watch the self-propelled vehicle go into action. That's Compton, I thought to myself an area that I once lived in and was my playgrounds. It has been a long time since I have been in that area, but, at UBER, we cannot refuse a client the right to be transported no matter what their origins are. Uber is an equal opportunity mobile transportation system. It did not take the vehicle long to reach the destination.

"You ordered a UBER" I asked, as the young lady, wearing pajamas she told me yes and wait just a minute as she went inside the little wooden house with a concrete porch. I waited and then, all hell broke lose.

"Get your shit out of here, you and the little ugly baby" I heard a man's voice shouting and the girl, I assumed, that just told me that she ordered a UBER, cursing and attempting to take the baby and a few Black Large Garbage Bags to the front yard.

"Oh my, G-Girl, what do I do, I was not taught how to handle a domestic dispute" I panic.

"Shall I sound the alarm?" said Google G-Girl.

"Yes, this can get ugly" Just as I responded, the girl ran out the house and there was this African American fellow beating her in the head. It will take time for the police to get here; so I must prevent the girl from being beat by this man.

""'Sir, stop it and let her go" As I jumped out of the Malibu and I was lucky my legs were on, but not as straight as I assumed.

"Oh, this is your boyfriend" the young black man said wearing a Dreaded Lock Hair Style.

"Look, we can resolve this problem before things get worst, the police are on their way" I called out.

"Police, you called the police, this is my bitch and my baby and you, you taking my girl away; you aren't even got a good arm; what are you going to do for her man"

"I am the driver-I drive for UBER"

"They let you drive without a arm"

"One good arm and no legs but I bet I can take you on fool"

"You aren't got no legs-wow, how you drive a car man"

"I don't, the car drives itself, and it is programmed by GOOGLE DRIVE"

"Man, my father had his legs amputated from the war, they train you guys to drive" The situation has cooled down somewhat, a good thing because I know I could not take on this Burly Big Nappy head Black Boy, but I was not going to let him beat her up either.

"There's a program that teaches veterans that are disabled to assist in the drive of UBER and that is what I do"

"Maybe my dad can do that-he is a veteran and he just sits around and watch television all day and on the week-ends plays domino's and cards at the Veterans American Legion"

"He sure can, that is, if he wants to do something different besides playing dominoes-now, I am going to take

Keisha to the address that on my destination drop off and the baby”

"Okay, take her, I will just wait for the police to come and arrest me for domestic abuse”

"Well, it does not have to be like that-all I got to do is call the dispatch and tell them that things are in control as long as you just go away”

"Okay, I will leave and Keisha, I will call you, and I am sorry baby-I will go over my father's house and tell him about driving UBER-what is your name”

"Mitchell Martinez, and this is my first day of driving-now, I will take her to her designated place; I assume it is her relative house” The baby, the two big trash bags and the Keisha got in the back seat of the car as I heard her crying as I got inside the UBER/GOOGLE car and placed my seat belt on and gave the command to G-Girl Google to drive to the designated drop off point.

"He said he will call you, so don't cry, things will get better for you and the baby-what is the baby name” I asked.

"Tasha” the young lady said as the vehicle drove off and the young man went walking down the street.

"Will I be taking you to your relatives house”

"Yes, my mother's house”

"Well, you will be better off there until things calm down with you and that young man”

"Thank you” she said.

"Your welcome” I told the young lady as we drove to Eighty-forth Street and Budlong off of Vermont Avenue. Her mother was in the front yard waiting as The UBER car must have sensed that the mother was interested in seeing her three month old granddaughter and her daughter brought home safely.

"Thank you mister, for all your help-Keisha told me what happened on her cell phone-what is your name"

"Mitchell Martinez maim, The UBER Driver"

"Your more than a Driver, you are a good man"

"Why thank you and take good care of the baby and your daughter" I said, as the mother asked me if I wanted something to drink and I said no thank you and continued to reprogram the computer and prepare for the next mission.

I resolved other incidents while in the war, assuring the local people in the villages that help from the United States Government was on it's way and the terrorist will not be back. I learned from my experience in the war and my experience that day on the streets; people are people no matter what nationality they are and they can be calmed down and told that things will be better, things will be better; just you wait and see….

Chapter IV

Grooving, On A Sunday Afternoon!

What a week I had as a UBER Driver; it was Sunday and I decided to take BU' my Malibu UBER car too the car wash and get it cleaned and tires shined up. That week alone there were over twenty clients with out a dull moment. What a difference a day made in the work force. My self esteem build up and I was able too communicate with people like no other time in my life. The President was right, a job helps building up one's confidence and helping the mind feel that there is some self worth in going out there and working for a living instead of receiving from the federal programs.

"Grooving, on a Sunday afternoon, that's my old song," I said to G-Girl after turning on the radio station to the oldie's but goodies. Reminiscing off the time that my friends and I use to go to the park and just lay in the grass and talk to the girls. Well, I have not seen or heard from those so-called friends in years. I guess they found out that I was injured in the war and gave me up for being dead. Well, the whole world has changed since the invention of the internet and all this other technology rushed in and what do we have now- kids that plug there ears with wires to listen to music and avoid communications with the outside world and computer programs that does everything but wipe your ass; well, technology will solve that event soon, why after all, they put a Man on the Moon.

With twenty-five passengers at the end of the week. The data shown that I received all one hundred twenty five gold stars, which made me a General in the eyes of the UBER accounts; the highest level of all UBER driver, according to the data from the accumulation of the statistics on my cell phone data list. All twenty-five passengers stated that cleanliness was regarded first and foremost. So why they did not rate me on my friendliness? I was always kind too them and went over my regular UBER job description in giving the passenger information on how to receive benefits, such as Veteran benefits; social security benefits and even to the young new mothers with babies I told them where the welfare office was to receive vouchers for baby formula. By now, I developed a keen eye on the buildings and all the signs of the city. Where health facilities are, businesses, hotels and restaurants.

Contributing my keen ability to be aware of everything in my surroundings to the incident that happened over fifteen years ago when my tanker truck, driving through a area where there were IUD explosives and all hell broke lose. It was a living hell and I suffered the lost of three of my extremities. Traumatized, but now I am aware of everything and everybody in my general surroundings.

Payday was on every Thursday and I need not go to the bank, they just deposit my weekly money straight into my bank account. This was an ideal thing for me since walking to the bank was too strenuous on my legs and waiting in line was tough. The people in line often stare at me and children come up to my wheelchair and look at the missing legs, gone from the knee caps and the Captain Hook arm scared the little one's as I use to tease them that I was Captain Hook and banished my steal prosthetic hand at them.

Everything was listed on the computer for the entire week of my driving. The mileage, the amount that UBER was paid and the amount that I received; including the cancellation fee of five dollars within the five minute limit and the Surge Time, which is the time that the demand for drivers are at it's most highest level. The surge time is the best time to drive and pick up passengers since the amount of miles paid can go up to four times the regular amount of one dollar per mile to four dollars per mile. The highest that I have ever witness Surge Time was Three dollars and seventy cent per mile. Now, I will pull up to the airport Cell Wait Lot and see if I can get a call to pick up at the local hotel or restaurants. At this time we were prohibited to pick up at the airports but we were allowed to drop off passengers at the airports.

"UBER Hum" A taxi driver came up to my vehicle and said.

"Yes, I drive for UBER-what do you need"

"What do I need, what do you mean what do I need, it is what do you need and how you drivers from UBER are taking our lively hood by picking up passengers that we would normally pick up"

"Excuse me-look, if you have a problem with UBER you talk to the UBER office, not me, I work like you work and I get paid for a job just like you do, so don't rant on me about UBER-You people that drive those Yellow Cabs should have been kinder to the people and should not have Price Gouged them for just driving them locally"

"How you know this-you are in this high tech UBER car and you are taking my money"

"Well your company should have updated your systems years ago and now, when there is a deficit in your clients, that is when you Taxi Drivers complain" I straight out told the taxi driver mohammed, since this was the news that I have been hearing from each and everyone of my passengers. How mean and ruthless the Taxi Cab drivers were and how dirty there taxi cabs were inside.

"You take this and this" Why you dirty son of a bitch, I said out load.

"What the F are you doing dude; you egged my car"

"Your car, it's a UBER car and it is taking the food and the rent money from my family"

"This is my car and I got the papers in my name you fool-G-Girl, set the alarm" I summons my system and told G-Girl, the GOOGLE System emergency alert to get help fast as I got out of my BU, my Malibu car that the government gave me, to stop this fool from throwing eggs on my car.

"You idiot, look what you have done to my car; it's black and you have ruin my car with egg yoke"

"Next time you will think before you take one of my customers"

"No, you will think before you assault my private property-look, here comes the Airport Security and they will arrest you for this" I told Mohammed.

"Arrest, for just throwing eggs on this UBER car"

"Yeah, you can't do that in this country, you have assaulted me and my property"

"You assaulted my family by taking food off our table" Here is the police now-"officer, look what he did too my car"

"This is your car sir"

"Yes and this Taxi Cab Driver egged it because I am a UBER driver officer"

"Well, we have been getting a lot of that lately-now tell me before I arrest this man, what is it with UBER that got the Cab Drivers so upset, The Limousine Driver so outraged and the transportation people rethinking their mode of transportation Sir" said the police airport officer.

"Price of Transport Officer"

"What do you mean-by the way, we viewed everything that this man did to your vehicle at our office and we were quick to respond"

"Okay, thank you; but the rates of using a UBER are way less than half of the rate of a Taxi and most UBER drivers are directly from the same community so we can have interesting conversations with our community members on what is happening in our own neighborhoods, while the Taxi drivers have an attitude about everything" I told the officer.

"That's not true- I live at the local hotel in the community and can not rent an apartment because of this man"

"Because of this man-why this man does not own UBER, he is just a driver like you are for the Taxi Company, but the only thing is, this is his vehicle that you have damaged and now you are liable sir"

"I am not Liable, he and UBER is Liable for taking the food from the mouths of my children and making us live in shabby and dope ridden hotels…UBER is the Devil…Ali… will curse UBER…" Said Muhammad, the Yellow, fear and Anger. Cab driver, which is too bad, since chances are he will be deported; that is, if I go to the airport security and press charges.

"Assa-Lamu-Alaikum, my brother and may UBER be with you" I told Mohammed the Cab Driver as they put him in the back seat of the patrol car and whist him away.

I won't press charges; it is only egg white and yellow yoke on my car. The yellow fear and anger is nothing compared to the outrage that Mohammed has for UBER and all he will be seeing is the white walls of a jail cell until The Yellow Cab Service come get him and his Yellow Cab from airport security.

"Thank you G-Girl, now, let's go to the park near by after I use these water bottles to wash the eggs off my car-why he must have had a dozen eggs to splatter on my machine"

"Time to get a wash" said the automatic GOOGLE signal on the dashboard as I commanded the vehicle to find the nearest car wash.

UBER is becoming a CULT on wheels. Me loving to just drive and the high adrenalin for the Game of the Greatest Catch. of The Day. Not many fish out there today; that is, I have not received a call pick up for at least thirty minutes. Very unusual for this time of day. I can get up to seven calls within a hour, all local and once I receive a airport run, all other calls are cancelled out.

There was big money in the airport run, since the LAX could take up to fifty minutes and at eighteen cent per minute that will be a handsome pay day on Thursday.

"Surge, at 1.00 x 3.70 cent per mile" the voice command rung out as the red light flashed but the calls for me to pick up remained dormant. What was happening is the Long Beach Marathon was taking place downtown Long Beach and the UBER drivers from here to San Diego, camp out, to make big money from the thousands of people that gather for events with limited amount of UBER drivers.

"BEEP, beep, beep" sounded out my Google system as I asked G-Girl.

"What we got G-Girl" Surging at $3.70 per mile, pick up at El Tortious, on PCH, Highway 1-your arrival time is 2:38, time of arrival"

"Okay, I got a catch, the passenger is on highway 1 at El Tortious but how will I get there with all these road closures due to the marathon?

"Your least traffic route is to take 2nd avenue to bellflower and make a left turn on Bellflower to pacific coast highway"

"Okay, the wheels are turning and I can see all the marathon runners-trotting to make it through the final goal line. Oh here I am-these two gals must be the pick up's.

"UBER, did you order a UBER ride?" I asked…

"Yes's" one of the girls said…

"Oh shit, there drunk"

"What took you so long UBER"?

"Well, I had to go all around since the roads were blocked-where you two headed maim" I asked, just too get some kind of as semblance on how drunk they are in order for me to have enough time to break out my towels in the back of my trunk so they can vomit on.

"This marathon is racking my brain-why, that is why we left home because of all the noise and all the roads blocked" blonde said, as the other brunette had trouble getting in her side of the car.

"You need help maim"

"No, I got it, wow, have you ever had Brunch at El Tortious man"

"No maim, I have not but what were they serving"
"Champaign dude"

"Really"

"Yeah and when we get home we are going to have another bottle of Champaign"

"Oh really" I said and kept my eye on them, since they did not appear that much drunk and they appeared to hold their own liqueur.

"Say, your cute, what are you" the brunette, slurring at the mouth and getting real lose in the back seat of the car as I commanded G-Girl to designate the pick up and called for the drop off point on the Google Maps.

"I am your UBER driver maim"

"I know that, I mean, are you from one of those Arab countries"

"No maim, I was born right here, that is, Los Angeles maim"

"You have such pretty cute curly hair and your complexion, it is like a Hershey candy bar. I love chocolate candy bars" She started putting her fingers in my hair and, that did not feel too bad, it has been a long time since I had that done by a woman.

"Why thank you maim-I will get you two home safely and try to avoid all the road blocks" I tried to change the subject as the brunette was aggressive while the blonde just kept watching and seemed to be a little upset.

"Oh, just run the barricade; why this is the only way we are going to get home, straight ahead" Blonde said.

Knowing people and these gals were on the borderline of being wasted, I just said!

"Well, why and the Hell not, let me just run right through this barricade and Thelma, Louise, you both put your seat belts on and here we go…"

"Awe" they laughed and yelled out and thought that I was really going to do it. The first thing the police would do is to take down the Black Man and Thelma and Louise will get home in time to pop open a bottle of Champaign and place the whole incident on their Facebook. I slowed down and took a left turn from the command that I gave G-Girl and the car slowed to a crawl, the Champaign Gals got home safely.

"Say, what are you doing now" they asked, while they were getting out the car.

"Just driving, that is until five o'clock this evening"

"Come on up and have a drink with us-we are celebrating the marathon"

"Well, I would love to join you ladies, but I got to work"

"Work, you're a UBER driver, you can turn off and turn us on all at the same time"

"Sounds good, but Thelma, Louise, have a toast for me your Five Star UBER Driver"

"You got our Five Stars because you are cute and you are professional"

"Good bye ladies, have a good Champaign Marathon…

"Wow, that was strange; This Is A Mobile Jerry Springer Show; On Wheels…UBER REALITY…

Chapter V

The Rider

Two and a half weeks as a UBER driver and two checks. I caught a sell and bought two pro-cam video cameras to place on the rear back panel and one in the front inside window, in the corner. Things were getting more and more dangerous for the UBER drivers. Being hit in the back of the head when asked to place a seat belt on and the other UBER driver being accused of kidnapping when the lady said she was locked in the car and lied about the driver was attempting to molest her. I wanted to protect my UBER Machine and myself. Although the Malibu was equipped with a frontal camera, I needed a system that could video tape take all that is going on with the passengers that left me vulnerable and the fact remain that I could not react as fast with one arm and no legs.

"Time to go on the early morning run G-Girl" as I left my place and it was pitched dark. I turned the system on by a remote key switch and I was ready to roll in a matter of minutes.

"G-Girl, find something jazzy on the XM system, I mean, some song to wake me up and get me moving" I told the system to do as I rolled through the corridors of Long Beach, the down town marina area at five o'clock in the morning.

"Beep. Beep…Beep." the Google maps, destination rung while I strolled the Long Beach Marina area off Ocean avenue.

"Accept" I programmed in the trip and noticed it was The Marriott Hotel near the Queen Mary.

"Set the destination time G-Girl" I called out the order.

"Destination time, 4 minutes; you are due to arrive at five minutes after five M" We were in total synchronization; UBER, the Google, G-Girl (The nick name I gave the Google automated system for driving and of course, the Satellite way up in the sky).

"Turn left in five hundred feet to Aquarium Parkway" I checked to see if the cell phone and my maps guide were giving me the correct route, which it was.

"Roger on that, I can see the Marriott from my location-G"

"Security gate at the Marriott Hotel, at The Long Beach Marina-please press the red button on the left to enter the gate-your passengers will be notified" Thank you, G, I informed my favorite friend and Seeing Eye devise.

"UBER" I asked the couple, waiting in the front of The Marriott Hotel.

"The John Wayne Airport in Orange County" the gentleman said.

"Yes sir"

"We have two bags, will they fit inside the truck of your car"

"Why yes sir-I will press the release button and the truck will open sir-just place the luggage inside the truck sir"

"There's the luggage, you place the suit cases in the truck, that is what I am paying you for" said the man.

"Walter, I dare you talk to the UBER driver that way-why the twenty dollars that we are paying him will not even move the needle on his gas gage, now you put the bags in the truck Walter" said the nice lady, wearing a nice blue skirt and a matching jacket; I assumed that they were there for a meeting and Walter must have had a little too much to drink.

"That's okay maim, I will get the luggage, no problem, just give me a minute too put my legs back on"

"Oh my God, Walter, you see what you have done, this man is disabled and yet, he is still trying to make a decent living for himself and probably trying to feed his family. I will get the luggage and place them in the truck Mister; you just sit still and I will place the two suit cases inside the trunk" She was very much disturbed and adamant about helping me.

"Oh, I am so sorry sir" She placed the two bags of luggage inside the truck of the car while Walter, her husband watched feeling so bad at the time; stepped up to the plate and held the trunk a little wider and tried to help the lady place the luggage inside the truck while I tried to place my legs inside the socket and place the braces on so the prosthetic legs would not come off when I stepped down, out of the vehicle.

"We are so sorry sir" the couple continued to tell me as I pressed the Google button that indicated that the passengers were picked up as the signal started the destination and gave me the route to travel with the least traffic.

"I apologize sir," said Walter, still slurring with his mouth as he continued to apologize to make up for the insults that he addressed to me, not knowing that I have two missing legs.

"No sir, that was my fault, I should have placed my legs on before accepting the mission; I apologize". I told Walter, the abbreviated passenger.

"Excuse me, but your name is Mitchell, that was the name on the Google information about the driver, is that correct"?

"Yes maim"

"Just call me Betty and as you know from your cell phone, this is Walter, my husband"

"How do you do, Walter, Betty and will you two be flying out of the John Wayne Airport this morning to what destination and time, may I ask"?

"The whole environment had changed and I used my most professional tactics to make the two feel more confortable after Walter, became so belligerent.

"Sir, I heard that you said mission, were you in the military, I mean, when you were injured" said Walter, now calming down a little off his morning binge.

"Yes sir" I only said, as I kept my eyes on my monitors that now alerted me to a traffic collision on the 405 freeway, so, this gave me the signal to use the alternate route in order to make it to the airport in time and have the two get to their destination.

"We will be taking the car pool lane Maim, Sir" I informed the passengers.

"If you do not mind me asking Sir, Mr. Mitchell, were you injured in the war" I said yes, again and after reprogramming the cell phone too inform the GOOGLE Maps that I will take the fast track route.

"Why yes, I suffered a injury of severity, with both legs and my left arm," I told the couple as they gasped...

"Walter, and just too think, you were so mean to this man and he fought for you and the country Walter, for freedom and you insulted him something terrible-now; you apologize Walter and get out your pocket book and make it beneficial for him, you hear me" said the lady in blue; who went from red in her face to a critical CODE BLUE in her behavior after hearing that I, after fighting for freedom, in a foreign country, come home just to be insulted by her husband Walter.

"Well, I did not know Betty" Walter said.

"You should never treat people bad like you do Walter, I have told you and told you several times and if you were not so drunk you would have seen that his arm was gone" said Miss Betty.

"Oh, I am deeply sorry, we are here, at the airport; here you are sir, I will get the luggage out; I am very sorry"

"We can not accept tips sir but I will contribute this money to the Paraplegic Veterans of America, under the directorship of Arthur Lyles, who if you call the Long Beach Veterans Hospital and ask for Arthur Lyles, he will mail you a tax deductible recite" I told the couple and they shook my one good hand and gave me the upmost respect. They were off to their destination, with Walter walking behind Betty, still disgusted while the Bell Hop took their luggage.

The Rider, from the Tupac song, got me back on my feet, sort of speak after that one. I only had one thing to say after I pressed the proper button for the twenty-seven mile trip in which UBER and I split the pouch and I received $13.67 after being insulted, and humiliated.

"The next client please G-Girl" I pressed the drop off and waited for another passenger at the Cell Phone Waiting area at The John Wayne Airport in Orange County, California....

The car Mobile Phone rung, it was Larry, my UBER Technician.

"Hello" I responded to the call.

"Mitch-how is things going with your UBER Driving"

"Well, I have my good days and my bad days- how are things going with you Larry"?

"Well, Carl and I have been recruiting more and more veterans to drive our new UBER GOOGLE Vehicles"

"Oh really" I said and it was as if, Larry and Carl, sensed that something was wrong.

"Is there a problem?" Larry said.

"What's going on Mitch"?

"Oh, hi Carl" I responded.

"Well, from the almost four weeks that have driven for UBER and used the GOOGLE applications to pick up, and drop off passengers....

UBER IS A MOBILE SWEAT SHOP FOR THE UBER DRIVERS, A GHETTO GEARED TRANSPORTATION SYSTEM FOR THE PASSENGER, WITH THE NICKLE AND DIME FARES, AND A DETRIMENT TO ALL THOSE PREVIOUS TRANSPORTATION COMPANIES THAT HAVE PAID DEARLY TO CUMMUTE PEOPLE, FOR YEARS, AND NOW HAVE GONE BROKE; A BANKRURPTED, DINASOUR THE YELLOW CABS" I told it like it was.

"What" said Larry?

"Oh my" said Carl, why, what happened Mitchell?

"No respect"

"Can you be specific"?

"Why yes Larry-you see, although the passengers tell me many, many stories on how they are treated bad by the Yellow Cab drivers, with their attitude and their high fee for taking the passengers to their destination; but the low fee's and the UBER passengers dispensation's and their attire; why it's a GHETTO FARE TRANSPORTATION SYSTEM LARRY, CARL" I SAID.

"Wow, look, you have been driving for a entire month now Mitchell; do you foresee that you will be continuing to drive for UBER, at this time?"

"Hell NO" I said emphatically, without any prejudice.

"Well, this is a shocking statement by you Mr. Mitchell Martinez; we have been gathering all the information from your mileage, your exemplary five star rating and the cleanness of you and your vehicle; we are completely dumb folded from what you are just telling us" both Larry and Carl were shocked, but they are not the drivers of this UBER thing, they are the technicians and their jobs were at stake unless something is done with the clientele of the passengers.

"So how do you think, at this time, things can change, things will improve for the driver and the passengers"

"They won't, there will be no changes, that is, unless the department of transportation investigates this Illegal Sweat Shop on Mobile Wheels" I told them and from the over one hundred passengers that I have served in the passed month, not one passengers even committed on how do the UBER Drivers make ends meet when we are not paid for our gas that we put into our vehicles, we are not paid for the maintenance of having oil changes and transmission and the regular wear and tear on our vehicles and in addition, we are treated the reverse on how the Yellow Cab Drivers treat the passengers, the passengers are taking it out on us, their prior experience with being late for their jobs; when in fact, we were there waiting, outside their pick up place, they over slept, but

THE UBER DRIVER IS BLAMED FOR ALL OF THEIR INADEQUACIES....

"Carl and I will be on the next plane back to the UBER/ GOOGLE headquarters to talk to you more about these problems Mitch"

"Well, okay, I don't see how just talking will help, but I will continue driving for UBER, until I no longer can commit" I told Larry and Carl and we disconnected.

The nerve of them, Larry and Carl, recruiting the unsuspecting Veterans to drive for UBER without contacting me; the Proto-Type, the first tested and trained UBER/ GOOGLE driver to complete the new billion dollars project. They should have stayed in contact with me before going to Washington, D.C. and addressing Congress and the United States Senate about these PARTNERSHIP that they have written contracts to recite and train paraplegic disabled veterans to drive their automated GOOGLE cars.

"Things have not changed, I have survived; the war, it was phony, no weapons of mass destruction; the veteran benefits, now all gone, with the trillions of dollars spent for fighting the wars and now the Veterans Hospitals and Rehabilitation programs, once again, ask the Veterans, the inactive military too sacrifice their very SOULS and drive these Mobile Sweat Shop Machines, risky attacks, humiliation and their pension checks; it is outrages.

Meanwhile....

"Larry"

"Yeah Carl"

"Are you thinking what I am thinking"?

"Why, what is that Carl" the two, on their way back to the UBER/GOOGLE headquarters in Santa Monica talked too each other on the plane back.

"Mitchell, why if he spills the beans on the problems with UBER/GOOGLE, there goes our jobs, our salary, our lively hood"

"Wow, you got a point there Carl-what are we going to do, it does not seem that Mr. Mitchell Martinez is the type that will broadcast the inadequacies of our program, do you think Carl"

"We can not take that chance, we are receiving Billions of Dollars from UBER, from GOOGLE, from The Federal Department of Transportation and now, one bad apple can spoil the entire basket of Veterans that we are training"

"Well, we will map out a strategy when we get back to the headquarters-you may have a point there Carl…you may be right…something, must be done…."

Chapter VI

Transference

Maybe I was too harsh on the UBER mission statement. After all, the low price of the fare and the poor are getting to their destination without paying a great deal of money. I often wonder how was UBER set up, as to, anybody can hop into your private car and you take him or her to a designated point. Why I heard that you could actually buy a UBER pass from Craig's List. In the past, Craig's list has been linked to the killing and kidnapping of women; that dating service that some men and women subscribe too. Desperate measures means desperated means of action. I will have to apologize to Larry and Carl of calling UBER and GOOGLE a Mobile Sweat Shop. It is, but it was not for me to say!

"Beep…beep". Called the Google cell phone system; a hit; I chose to accept, so I geared up the system and launched The BU, Mobile-the city of Tustin, in Orange county; I am to pick up a Sue, so hear I go…

The 405 freeway to the Garden Grove 22 freeway and off on Brookhurst. As I thought to myself, this is the furthest pick up that I have ever had. Why I was in Long Beach and now I am driving all the way back to Orange County…

"Give me some beats G-Girl, wake me up, this time of the morning" I summons my help The G-Girl, and her automatic audio system and I accepted The Heat station on XM radio. Boy were they bumping that morning and it did not take me long at all as I looked and looked for the correct address as G-Girl gave me the signal that I have reached my destination.

"Say, here we are"

"Oh, I did not see you-now where you headed"

"639 Tustin Avenue"

As I asked the lady was with, you are Sue"

"No" she said as I thought to myself, here I go again"

"So where is Sue, her name is on the manifest"

"That's my sister-in-law" After I took a good look at the large gentleman, he was from a Hispanic background and he was carrying two large bags while the girl he was with had one bag. I popped the truck and they placed the luggage in the truck. I introduced myself and pressed the Start Button and let UBER/GOOGLE do the driving for me to the clients destination.

Not a long trip, just a few miles off the 22 freeways; I checked my gadgets and I was nearing my designated point.

"No, man, this is not the right place; take a right at the corner and go straight"

"Well it says 639 Tustin avenue on the destination point; the drop off point"

"Oh, that must have been a mistake; keep driving until you get to Westminster Avenue" He said, as the girl kept moving around and twisting as if she was nervous-something was up…

"Keep driving Sir" I asked politely, knowing that the two were tweeter's' those that partake in using Methephinemines (Speed) that causes them to behave sporadically-twisting, turning and moving inside my back seat.

"Keep driving Sir" since I noticed that I was going in circles as I continued to drive, stopped, for a minute and see if the place was correct, as I could see that someone was waiting inside the office, as they walked out and was handed something; I assumed it was drugs.

"Okay, you two have a good morning" I told them, because after driving for an hour, going from one place to another-it was time for them to get out of my car.

"Take us to Golden State Boulevard man and that is where we will get out"

"Okay sir, Golden State and what?

"Bolsa Chico" Wow, that is a long way from where I am now-I got to find the police and get them out of my car-I thought to myself.

"No, no, no; I tell you what, just take us back to 639 Tustin Avenue, let me use your cell phone Boss"

"My cell phone, you can't use my cell phone, it is only for the dictation of my voice, it can not take and compute your commands"

"Look Jose, he aren't got a arm" As I turned my body toward them to explain that this system is not for the public use, I must have spooked them with a stainless steel arm that looked like a Captain Hook Hanger that will tear there throats out real quick…

"Okay Boss, let us out, right here, right at this hotel, on the left" He started speaking something in Spanish as I made a left turn and pulled into this Hotel and Low and Behold, it was the same Hotel: 639 Tustin Avenue that was on the manifest-Boy do I have a Guarding Angel.

Made, a pretty healthy purse that time; noticing the payout of over $100.00 dollars for the over one hundred miles of a fiasco that could have ended up deadly.

They got out there bags and left my sight as I turned off the system completely. I made a vow to myself years ago, that I would not ever place myself in another position to be Killed Again…I broke my Vow when, not knowingly, picked up some Meth Dealers and drove them all throughout Orange County, not knowing there names, to which they come from, to where there true destination and their background. The same position in which I lost my legs and my arm; not knowing, not knowing; just like the position I was placed in during the war, not knowing, not knowing…. with UBER not ever knowing nothing….

Orange County, the land of the new generation, why, as I can see from the now daylight, it is a very new developing area, why The Old El Toro Air Base use to be right over to the left on El Toro Avenue and Saddleback. I can remember the time when, while in the military, we use to have maneuvers there right there where they kept that Aircraft Hanger. Now just a memory and a lot of homes. I hope they destroyed all those underground evacuation bunkers at the El Toro Marine Base. The base was originally built during World War II and the invasion of Pearl Harbor when Franklin D. Roosevelt, the President, restructured the entire Marine Core because of the Bombing of Pearl Harbor, the bombs and ammunition to fight the Japanese had to be stored away from Hawaii, just for safety reasons. I hope they took those bombs out of those underground bunkers…

Beep…beep…

We got a hit. I accepted.

El Toro Road off of Jamboree Road; 15000 Laguna Valley Road-said the G-Girl, as I gave the command to start the destination and proceed to pick up the client.

Such a beautiful landscaping, way to serene for a military base; now there are home and children going back and forth to school, walking on their own with their big book bags, so big, that you can barely see the little toddlers. Now I am proud to have served in the Military, sacrificing my life just too see these young people walking to school, independently, getting their education and striving in The American Way. Why this road leads to a school; well, G-Girl has never given me the incorrect address yet. After over one hundred passengers, GOOGLE has never gone, wrong…

"UBER" I heard a voice, calling the UBER name.

"UBER-right over here-here we are" What is this, a High school and children, High School Students calling out the UBER name, summons me, there has got to be a mistake.

"UBER, wait, I ordered a UBER Car" the young lady said.

"You, why you ordered a UBER car-what is your name"? I asked her.

"Elaine"

"Well this manifest says Laine, not Elaine," I told the young lady.

"That's my mother, I use her account to be driven home from school"

"School is not out yet, school is still in session, why it is only 1 o'clock p.m., you better go back to class young lady," I told her very politely.

"No, wait, I got out of class early, you see, there is a teachers meeting so they let us leave early today.

"Well, are you eighteen years of age"?

"Yes" she said.

"Let me see your Identification"

"I left it at home"

"Young lady, I can't take you away from the school premises without the permission of your parents, I am sorry"

"What the hell" the young girl said, to my total surprise.

"Young lady, you should not talk like that"

"You mean too tell me I been waiting all this time for a UBER Driver too come and pick us up and you say you are not going to drive us"?

"Sorry, against policy rules"

"I have been driven out of here many times before you came here, you dam, N________er'…

"Now I am not going to sit here in my car and listen to you bad mouthing me young lady-and you said when I first asked you that the teacher let you out early because of a teachers meeting but yet still, you told me that you have been waiting for a long time-now what is it"

"You dam idiot, wonder you're just a UBER Driver, you don't know shit-I am going to report you too UBER"

"Okay, my name is Mitchell"

"Mitchell, the one arm bandit, you handicapped Black son-of-a-bitch"

"Good bye" I drove off, but, that girl has got to be reported, her foul mouth and she was leading out those other girls from school, eager to jump into my back seat to go to some kind of a ditch school party I bet. I am going to the principle's office, this sort of thing must be reported before one of these girls come up missing, dead in these here canyons.

I parked and took off my UBER sign out of the front window so those bad little girls would not identify me at the other end of the parking lot of the High School. I tighten up my legs with the twisted bolts on both sides and proceeded to walk toward the Principles Office.

"Excuse Me," I said, as I stepped to the receptionist desk.

"Yes sir, can I help you" the receptionist responded.

"I am a UBER driver and this young lady, presumably one of your students scheduled a UBER driver, me too pick her up"

"What" the receptionist yelled out as I was surprised and thinking to myself, once again, my intuition must have served me correctly.

"Here is the Principle sir"

"Yes, hello, my name is Mitchell Martinez and I am a UBER driver and one of your students, a female, ordered a UBER ride but I refused too pick her up"

"What is that students name, did you get her name," the principle, now getting irritated said.

"Irene or Rene"

"Oh my gosh, she is up too her old tricks again-and your name again, Mitchell, Martinez"

"Well thank you very much Mr. Martinez, I am going to call security and call her parents immediately; you see Mr. Martinez, Rene, is one of the schools biggest trouble makers and she has been expelled several times for her charades and now, this is it, I want to thank you very much"

"Well, don't be too hard on her-she is only a child and children must learn, hopefully, before it is too late"

"Well, we will take that into consideration but in the mean time my secretary has already got her mother on the phone; once again, thank you and have a nice day sir"

"You too, good-bye" Wow, I knew she was trouble with that big foul mouth of hers'. Better too learn now before it is too late to correct some of her problems. That girl is like one of those bombs that were stored in those bunkers at El Toro Air Base ready to go off any minute, but not on me, this time....

That IUD, taught me one thing; no matter how big or how small the substance is; whether it be human or a rock, don't trust it; keep your head up and your arms away from little girls that carry bombs. That is what got me out of the war, a little innocent girl strapped with explosive by the terrorist that blew the Hell up of my tanker petroleum vehicle. It appeared to be an innocent girl but she knew what to hit and she knew when and where the convoy was traveling too. Be aware of the young!

Done for today, homeward bound G-Girl; play that Tupac track for me, THE RIDER....

""Did you say, The Rider"

"Yes"

"Okay, The Rider, by Tupac Shakur, will be programmed for your listening pleasure-Have a Safe trip back home; Good Bye...

All system shut down, for today....

Chapter VII

Review of the Mission

Back at the UBER/Google Headquarters in Santa Monica, California.

"Has it been two months since I have been here and graduated from UBER School"

"Time passes by and now we have over fifty UBER drivers, just like you Mitch, willing, able and ready to drive their new UBER Machines," said Larry, while Carl, flanged him from his side as I looked at all the technicians and mechanics preparing new UBER/GOOGLE vehicles for the road.

"You're the man Mitch-The UBER GROOVER MAN" Larry and Carl Joked

""That I am, I am the UBER Man, with me, the entire system stands, at my very hands…

And I am so much in demand, well, Gosh Dam; with my five star rating, no one can touch me, with my Malibu UBER Car, no one dares brush me, yes, I am the Man, let these rookies try and catch me, if they can"

"You been tuning into XM radio Mitch, listening to those RAP Songs"

"How you know that"

"Just listening to your rymms, that were right on time, I knew, you were listening too The New View on XM radio too… tune in all the time and that is why Larry and I rhymes…

52

"OH, you two are good. So tell me, what is happening with the project"?

"Well, we got big contracts but not enough shoes to fill those demands"

"The turn over rate is high; we train them, we furnish them a new UBER/GOOGLE mobile and after two to three months, they vanished, quit and we got to take back their vehicle"

"Is that right Carl"?

"We have a high turn over rate-it is a serious problem Mitch"

"All you guys do is pay them the minimum wage, by the hour, not descent wages and I guarantee you they will stay with the program-you see my past two months manifest; I had over twenty cancellations and it was over five minutes after I accepted the call and I was on my way to pick the passenger up and my gas, my time and my vehicle had to be reprogrammed; I lost big time on all twenty of these cancellations"

"Take that into consideration Carl; we will talk to the UBER/GOOGLE Board of Directors about that issue"

"What good will that do Larry, I try calling and I write the UBER Support System and all they tell me is that they will get back with me and they never do-I never get the five dollars for the cancellation and I only get a high ass Gas Card Bill from all those cancellations and the gas I just waste"

"The UBER system will change, just you wait and see Mitch. Things will get better; we must have more drivers for these machines to work; it is required by California vehicle law; there must be a person under the wheel at all times"

"If not, what will happen when the technology gets so advanced that the Department of Transportation passes a new law in California excluding the driver, in small communities for their airport run, a driver is not even required, what happens then-a whole lot of drivers will be out of a job"

"How is your machine running Mitch" said Larry and I knew what he was getting too, you see, I made sure that I received the so called "Pink Slip" to my Baby-BU, my Malibu is mine and they must have found out-a little glitch that I noticed in the contract that the federal government, who was in a Contract with General Motors, provided for me since I am a disabled wartime veteran-the car was given to me as a Vocational Rehabilitation equipment gift. That was a smart move on my part.

"When they totally automate the system there will be a lot of drivers upset, right Mitch" said Carl.

"Yeah, I guess; driving for UBER is no job that you can rely on anyway; it all depends on how many people take the car or drives that determine how much the driver is paid, and that is not a good deal, right Carl"

"Yeah, your right, but we will fight for the drivers and get them a pay raise and benefits"

"Well you better do something, there is talk about Unionizing and I hear talk about STRIKE in the air"

"Oh no, that would ruin us, the whole system will fail unless those CEO's get their Fifty Billion Dollars a Year off those intakes from the drivers" Carl slipped and told me how much the UBER President made. Now in over 300,000 communities, world wide; the faucet is flowing but the unions will shut that faucet off in a heartbeat....

"Time for my doctors appointment-talk to you fellows later" I told the team and then proceeded to my BU, where the engine was already running.

Fifty billion dollars and those CEO's are using us drivers to fill their bank accounts, that aren't right-now, what did I do with that Union representative card; maybe I will give him a call, this shit has got to come to an end. No pay, just a partnership with UBER! That don't mean nothing when you got bills to pay and rent and food to put on the table-I will join the Union....

"There's a lot of wear and tear on your knee, scraping and it looks like lesions-now, what are you doing these days besides driving for UBER Mr. Martinez" said the Orthopedic Prosthetic Physician.

"Walking doctor, I walk and carry the passengers bags and I load their bags and sometimes, carry their bags into the airport for them"

"But why, you have been set up with a job that does not require all of that; all that you are required to do is pick up and drop off-you are not required to carry any bags and load and unload suit cases" said Dr. Cheng, my long time prosthetics, orthopedic surgeon who helped design my legs and my arm for me to have more mobile ability (Movement).

"I will not feel right if I can not help my passenger with their journey to their destination"

"But it is wearing you out Mr. Martinez; you will soon have an infection in your right leg and I can see that your cloths are wearing out by some kind of rubbing your knees on your cloths with your prosthetic steel screws in the way"

"That's the under dash when I drive, I rest my leg on the under dash of the dash board; it give me comfort when the rattling comes from the under dash and it is like having a message with all those high technological instruments on my dash panel"

"Well if you keep that up you will have to have a new prosthetic leg built; you are tearing off the plastics and the screws are loosening, the treads are being stripped" Doctor Cheng said, as I realized that UBER, is getting the best of me and with the more than 400 passengers that I try to serve with the upmost courtesy and professionalism, I am being drained, used, exploited and "Sweated Out" by driving people for six dollars and eighty-seven cent, on their pool manifest for twenty miles one way and I got to pay for my ticket back to my destination.

Leaving the doctors office at The Veterans Medical Center, I became depressed; is this what I dam near died for; for this UBER organization to come into my life and exploited me, my physical ability and "Cash In" on the unknowing, the Unwitting and the people that have been deprived and exploited for their driving abilities. Well, I can quit, I can resign, I do not have too continue driving, do I?

What a rush, driving; I can smell the fresh air when my window is down, I can roll with the best of them in my 2016 UBER Mobile and the community give me prompts; they respect Their UBER drivers, they love their UBER DRIVERS for as a UBER Driver this is their only way out of these deprived, debilitating and non-communicative environments-I SET THEM FREE, FOR LITTLE OR NO MONEY....

"BEEP, beep beep."

"Oh darn it, I forgot to shut down my system, since after my doctors appointment, I was going to drive back home and call it a day; oh well, I never refused a patron-I will drive them anywhere they want me too; I will enjoy their conversation and I will continue to give them my suggestions-I am addicted now too driving for UBER. I am a UBER Groover...."

"Hollywood G-Girl"

"Your pick up will be on sunset and vine M"

"Okay, let's role; we are working late this evening for the first time, but, what the heck; it may be a interesting venture"

"You will reach your destination at 7:38 p.m. and I will direct you to the route with the least traffic M"

"Thank you G-Girl" I responded, never knowing that G-Girl would probably not know what I just said, well, anyway; it is good company just to be with G-Girl, the Gal that never disputes me and never gives me a sassy comment.

"You have reached your destination, your destination is on the right"

"Why this is a ladies of the night, vanity shop, what the hell is going on G"?

"This is the destination placed in the system Mr. M"

"Okay, have the client, this Spice girl, been notified that I am here waiting in the parking lot, of this Porno Place"

"Your client has been notified"

"Here she, oh my G, she is beautiful-what kind of a beautiful woman would be here, in Hollywood, at this Porn Tool place"

"UBER"

"Yes maim, can I take you to your destination"

"Why yes, what a nice car you have Mr. UBER"

"Oh, that is not my name maim, my name is Mitchell"

"I know that, I read it on the profile-so, did the program, I mean, my destination go through okay"

"Yes maim; highland and San Vincentia, that is where your destination will be according to the screen maim"

"Stop calling me Maim, call me Spice-isn't that what it says on your cell screen"

"Why yes, but is that your real name"

"Why it most certainly is Mr. Mitchell"

"Okay maim, we are off to your destination, and I have programmed my UBER/Google phone".

"What happened to your left arm" Oh man, she saw it, my arm; I tried to shield it but I guess it came out just like my privates are throbbing with this smell good, taking sexy and the most beautiful women I seen in a long time.

"The war Miss Spicy, I was wounded in the war"

"Oh, poor baby, say, what nationality are you-you have the most beautiful hair-curly and locked, you are very handsome, does the military make you drive for UBER"

"Well, you can say that Spice"

"Say, how long are you working tonight, I have some aged wine up at my place-let's have a drink; why this is the week of the Veterans, isn't it"

"That's Veterans Day Spice and yes, it is on Monday, the celebration for Veterans Day"

"You can come up and have a drink, can't you"

"Oh, why, okay, I will have a drink with you since you insist, after all, it is Veterans Day, a Celebration for what the Veterans have done to secure freedom, isn't it"

"Yes, it is and I would love to have a drink with you and show you how much I appreciate what you and all the veterans have done for us"

"Maim"

"Call me Spicy"

"Okay, Spicy-I want to inform you that not only is my left arm prosthetic, so are my legs up to the knees"

"Oh, poor baby, can you walk to my door or will I have to carry you"

"No maim, I mean Spice, I have prosthetic legs, legs made for me to walk, just like every body else walks-I can manage"

"Well, here we are; you can park in my under ground parking stall, here, let me let you inside the security gate"

"Okay" How can I resist her; it was like the beauty and the beast-she was sentimental and patriotic and the one invitation this late evening that I was not going to refuse…I turned the system off and we both walked to her apartment.

Chapter VIII

The UBER GROOVER putting his thing down!

"Nice place" I said, as I sat down on Spice's leather coach"

"It will do for just me" she said as she broke out two crystal glasses and went to her kitchen to get a bottle of Chardonnay wine.

"So Michelle, how do you like driving for UBER" as she placed the glasses on the glass table and poured the wine into both the glasses.

"UBER is not the job I would want to make a career of," I told her.

"That's what I have been hearing from the UBER drivers that I used in the past-they told me that UBER is good for the passengers but bad for the drivers" Boy was she sexy as she walked around to the other side of the coach and sat near me as we sipped on some wine.

"I guess it is okay too drive for a part time job but it does not pay enough, there are no benefits and you got to buy your own gas-that's not fair at all"

"So why are you working for UBER" "It is the Chase of the Game, the thrill of driving and meeting other people is what I enjoy"

"Oh really, well you're a people's person, I assume"

"UBER, got me out of my shell" "Your shell, so you were having problems" she asked, as he got a little closer as if she was analyzing me.

"Look at me, one arm and two prosthetic legs; sure I was depressed, for a number of years but now, since I have been meeting people, people that care about us disabled veterans, things have gotten better in my life"

I don't see why people would be so mean toward the veterans; my brother went to war and he had some mental issues and he committed suicide after taking all that medicine that those doctors gave him-it ran him crazy"

"Yeah, you got to be careful when your taking those drugs-you will lose it real quick"

"Have you ever lost it"?

"No, never have, I had nothing too lose" She laughed and thought I was funny; it was the wine working in my favor as she got lose and put on some music.

"So, you have a nice place and you are very attractive-just what do you like to do when you're not working"?

"Oh, I like going to the movies and visiting museums and stuff like that; oh, I like traveling also"

"So do I, I like movies and going to the museum but after the war, I haven't had much of a desire to travel" "Why not"

"Well, my legs-it is too inconvenient to be pushed in a wheel chair and the transportation system is terrible when it comes to loading and unloading a electric wheelchair"

"How long have you had the prosthetic legs"?

"For about six months-they work okay but it took some time to get use to, you see, they have electronic sensors and I can move my legs just by using my thought pattern-they work as if they were real legs"

"That's good, you mean to tell me that you can make your legs move by thinking of something in your head"

"Sure, watch this-I am sitting down and now, I want to move my leg to get up, so I think about it and my legs follow the command from my brain"

"Wow, the things that they are doing with science now a days"

"So what type of work do you do Spice" I finally asked her.

"I work in a club"

"A where house"

"No, I work in a club serving people and dancing"

"So you are a dancer"

"Some what"

"So you are a waitress"

"Some times-now you have one more guess"

"A stripper"

"Yes" How did you guess?"

"Well, I picked you up at a Novelty shop on Hollywood Boulevard and with a body like that, I put two and two together"

"Wow, you are nice, do you object to a lady being a stripper"

"Some what, I feel that there are other occupations that a girl can have to make a living"

"Well, I do not plan on working at the strip club long, just to finish my beautician school and I will one day set up my own shop"

"So you're going to school to be a beautician"

"Yes; I have a part time job also; I dress up the dead at the mortuary-I fix their hair and apply make up to the dead people"

"That does not bother you"

"It use too but I got use to it; the dead can not hurt you like some people can"

"No, I mean being a stripper-that does not bother you when you have to entertain men for money"

"I only strip down to the breast, not the goodies"

"So you work at a topless bar"

"Yes, they have drinks at the topless bar and I make big tips"

"Do you have a boyfriend" I just had to ask her.

"No, I use too but he could not get use to the late hours of me working and he was insecure and always thought that I was seeing someone at the Club-we broke up"

"OH"

"How about you, do you have a girl friend"?

"A girlfriend, now what girl would want me"?

"Your very handsome, very good looking and women should look beyond your disability and accept you for who you are"

"Well that is the nicest thing I have heard in a long time-say, now I know how you deal with putting on make up and fixing the hair of the dead people-you look beyond their deadness"

"Your so funny"

"So are you, well, I guess I will be getting back to Long Beach"

"Long Beach, you got too drive all the way back to Long Beach after drinking-why you can get some rest on my coach and leave in the morning"

"I can"

"Sure, I trust you, you seem like you are a nice person to be friends with"

"Okay, all I need is a sheet and a pillow and a blanket and I will crash right here on your coach-thank you Spice"

"My real name is Silvia-I did not want to give you my real name until I got to know you better-some men are ruthless"

"I understand-you learn a lot working at the Club and working on the Dead, don't you"

"Yes, I do, everyday"

"I learned a lot working for UBER" Silvia gave me a blanket, a pillow and a sheet to lay on her coach but, I did not get a chance to sleep on the coach; she was lonely and I sensed it so I got in the bed with her and the rest is HISTORY....

Smelling the aroma of bacon aroused me, as I opened my eyes and looked throughout the room to observe a very neat and well-organized set of furniture. My prosthetic legs were placed on the side of the bed and the girl has so much concern, she made sure that my legs were in my reach. My arm was still attached, for logistical reason, I would imagine; thank heaven she did not have an air mattress or waterbed. Everything seemed in tack.

"Do you like your eggs scrabbled or sunny side up" said Sylvia, wearing a silk see through robe.

"You fixed breakfast" I asked, as I pushed my way to grab my legs and attached them so I could come to the living room and the kitchen to see what was going on. I had not slept so well in over twenty years.

"Sure, I thought that you would be hungry and I got up and started breakfast for us-I laid out a towel and wash cloth so you can shower-do you need help"

"Oh, no, these prosthetics are plastic and water proof, I can use them just as I would use my real legs, if I still had them" I told Sylvia as I went went toward the bathroom and there was even a cloth rob for me. This girl really had a lot of class. I wondered where she was from, since, in my hay day, I did have a few women but none like this one; she was right on time. Before I could think about doing something, she would have already had the same idea and handled it.

"Are you UBERING TODAY"

"Yes, I plan on working my way too Long Beach, picking up passengers on my way back home"

"Are you going to make your way back here tonight"?

"Oh yeah, I will be back-what time do you got to be at work"

"School today, I have classes and a test on all the nerves of the head-I am almost finished with my beautician classes and ready to take the exam to become a beautician"

"That's great Silvia-I know you will do well in your new career-the food smells and look so good, wow, are you sure that your not graduating from Culinary School"

"My grandmother taught me how to cook, that's the first thing that us Georgia Girls had to learn is to cook and clean, it was mandatory before we left home to go into the world"
"Your from Georgia-why I have been there, Fort Benning Georgia where I went to 'Jump School' in the Airborne-nice place to live"

"I am from Atlanta, Georgia and I sure do miss my family and friends"

"Well maybe you can go back and visit after you graduate from school"

"Maybe I will but what will you do when I leave"? Wow, I feel cupid's arrow. From just the little things that she says and the things that she does, make my stomach have

Butterflies. Oh boy, I got to think this one out and come up with a remedy for Love Potion Number Nine.

I showered up and made it to the breakfast table and the scrabbled eggs were so fluffy and light and the bacon fixed thoroughly, all the way through, brown and well done. Just to think, I was about to reject this assignment and go back to Long Beach. I would have missed my Soul Mate and my life would have been incomplete. I decided that I would take a day off from driving UBER and I took Sylvia too school and hung out with her after she got out of her class. We came back to her apartment after shopping for me some cloths and under wear and a tooth brush and I knew that this little round the view would turn into a permanent Love Affair.

Chapter IX

UBER/GROOVER'S

Six months have expired and driving for UBER changed my entire life. Now that I have a girlfriend, that has become my fiancé" and I have moved into her place; driving for UBER, the economical transportation system has made me a new man, from a depressed Veteran to a Self confessed Man. Not even the therapist could get the information from me about my ordeal and accident that happened during the war, but Sylvia could. We became so close, that I decided to ask her for her hand in marriage.

"Do you think that your parents will accept me?" I asked Sylvia, as we boarded a plane headed for Atlanta, Georgia so that I would meet her family.

"Why wouldn't they accept you, my people are not phony, besides, my father was injured in Viet-Nam; he is like you"

"Like me, what do you mean like me Silvia"?

"Well, I don't talk about the hardships and other people's life, but my brother committed suicide from coming back from the war and he could not live up to my father's expectations-My father is a Lifer from the Marine Corp and he had his foot amputated, but his injury happened after he retired from the military; he is a diabetic"

"Oh. Now I see what you mean-that's understandable, you not telling me about your family-I understand; you know nothing about my family and there is probably nothing to tell"?

"Come on, our plane is boarding-it is a good thing you have that TSA exclusive boarding pass; with those steel legs and arm, they would have had you strip down to your underpants"

"Titanium, not steel, the screws and the shafts are titanium and those detectors do not go off when I pass through them Missy"

"Oh, good-look, I was not trying to be sarcastic, just inquisitive Matt"

"Yes. I know and that is one thing that we did not talk about, my prosthetics"

"Well, we will have time to do all that once we get to Atlanta and settle into my parents house"

"Do they have UBER there"?

"UBER, well, I guess they do, I haven't heard anything about UBER but I imagine they have a taxi service at the airport-why Matt, we reserved a car at the airport"?

"I was just wondering"

"Oh no Matt, your not going to go back to driving UBER in Atlanta-your on vacation and this may turn out to be our honeymoon-we got to safe money and I don't want you working for that UBER long"

"Why, what is wrong with UBER" "Matt, you talk about UBER all the time, everyday when you get off work, now I want you too relax and enjoy me and my family; I have a few places that I want you too visit with me; historical places'

"Oh yeah, I want to go to The Martin Luther King Memorial and Fort McPherson"

"There is no more Fort McPherson Matt-it is Fort Medea-Tyler Perry bought the entire Army Fort and turned it into a Movie Studio"

"Really; yeah, maybe I can write a play, a screenplay about my experience with UBER"?

"Now Matt, we made a deal, an agreement that if I quit my job at the Club, you would not always talk about that UBER-your days are numbered with UBER anyway"?

"What, what do you mean my days are numbered with UBER; I have worked for UBER for six months, it is not a hard job, just the people are three degree's of In-Sanity, Sometimes Silly and Stupid; 3 degree's of Separation-now how am I going to support you without working for UBER"

"Matt, you have a pension and you have a education, now, those applications that you have sent out, I am sure something will come through for you, real soon besides driving all day for that UBER company"

"Maybe-all we can do is hope for the best"

"Yes, and let's enjoy ourselves while we are in Atlanta"

"Okay" She won again, why she had my whole life planned for me; this girl will take good care of me but leaving UBER, I don't know; UBER is a MOBILE CULT, once your in it, your Hooked, On Driving....

"Good to meet you Mr. Williams, Mrs. Williams" I so politely said as I entered the entry of their beautiful home in Briarwood; a suburb of Atlanta, Georgia.

"OH, he is a fine looking man Sylvia-what are you anyway" said Mrs. Williams.

"Pardon me Maim"? I did not understand what she meant.

"Momma, he is African American, just like we are Momma" said Sylvia.

"I have never seen no Black Man with hair like that-is your momma White"

"Oh, no sir-my mother was from The Oklahoma Indian Tribe-Chiquita and my father was Louisiana 'Creo' Sir"

"So you a Indian"

"No sir-I am African American Sir"

"So, how you get that Martinez name, it sounds like a Mexican name"

"My family migrated from Spain sir, on my father's side and from what I have found out, the original name was Martin, but the clerk at the records hall during the slavery era, miss-spelled the name on my great grandfather's birth certificate from Martin to Martinez"

"Oh, they messed you up like they did a lot of us"

"Daddy, now, enough for all the prodigy stuff, Mitchell name is Mitchell Martinez and he is just like we are, African American" said Sylvia, at this time disgusted with her mother and father drilling me, but, that was okay; I expected that; just wait until they see my legs and one arm, they will really freak out.

We then took our luggage to our room upstairs in the split-level home. What a beautiful house and the thing that I could not understand was how did a beautiful girl from Atlanta, Georgia, move to Hollywood, California and become a Stripper when her parents are well to do?

"This was my room Mitch and across the hall was my brother's room and my baby sister room is across the hall"

"So you have a sister"

"Yes, she just moved back, she will be here soon, in time for dinner"

"So your brother, he is no longer with us"

"No, he was all messed up from the war and killed himself; that room of his has never been touched since he killed himself inside there-he was a veteran"

"Oh, I am sorry to here that"

Junior, tried to get help, but by then it was to late and he hung himself right inside that room there-my parents never went back inside that room after that happened"

"How long ago was that"?

"Oh, about five years, Oscar Junior, was the oldest" I could tell that Sylvia was sad and did not want to talk about the death of her brother, but what I could surmise, the oldest brother, took care of his parents very well after his demise from this beautiful home from the suburbs of Atlanta, Georgia.

"This is my room, just the same as it was when I left"

"Cute-but, I would rather stay in a hotel; you know what we do best at night and with your parents room just down the hall way-well, they might hear us"

"Sorry Mitchell, but you will have to sleep in the guess room"

"The what"

"The guess room-down stairs in the basement"

"What do you mean" "Oh, we are not married yet so, my parents suggested that you sleep in the guess room-it is nice down there with a bed and a bar and a pool table and a large flat screen television"

"I don't care how nice it is, you will not be beside me"

"Wait until you see it-it is a Man Cave in the basement" said Slvia"

"Let's get a hotel room honey, I will not be able to sleep without you"

"We got to save our money Mitch since, well-I was not sure, but I guess it is safe to tell you now, I am pregnant"

"What" I was shocked; I thought that she was acting peculiar, going to the bathroom a lot an her complexion of her face changed-she is having a baby-our baby, that is why she wanted to come home and get all of that motherly advise-wow, I was taken back for a few minutes and then I thought to myself-since I only have a half of a arm and stubs for legs, how will the baby turn out" Well, I think that the injury was not a congenital injury so it was not genetic, so, the baby will be okay, but how am I going to play with the baby with these legs and a captain hook fingers. I could not worry about all of that; I had to take care of Sylvia now and make sure she get all the nutrition she needs, she is eating for two now.

"Sylvia" I heard a voice call out, now trotting up the stairs.

"Oh, it is my sister, Salvo" "Salvo, are you two twins"

"No, but…" she, oh here she is" Dam, her sister was as beautiful as she is!

"Sylvia, it is so good to have you home again"

"It is good to be back girl-you look like you have gained a little weight"

"Just a little, but I am working out now"

"Sister, this is Mitchell, my fiancé'"

"Momma said he is good looking; are you two going to have children"

"Salvo, we only been seeing each other for six months"

"It only takes a moment and, well, before you know it, momma will be a grandmother," said Salvo.

"Yeah-momma will be a grandmother" they would not let me get a word in as I just listened and watched these two sisters-they have a lot in common.

"So Mitchell, when is the big day"

"Oh, the marriage, well, any time now, maybe on this trip"

"You all getting married here, in Atlanta"

"Salvo, now look what you started"

"That may not be a bad idea, since all of your family will be here for the reunion-we can have the military chaplain marry us, right here in Atlanta"

"There is not enough time to plan nothing Mitch, the reunion is next week and we got to get license and blood test"

"They can do that at the Military Base"

"The military base, well they closed that one down-were you in the Military, Mitchell"?

"Yes I was"

"You look awfully young to have retired, our daddy retired a Master Sargent-what was you rank"?

"A Sargent"

"Really" said Salvo.

"You see; I was injured during the war Salvo"

"My dad said he was injured too, but he does not like talking about it"

"Well, it use to bother me, but now that I have accepted my injuries, I say: Get Over It, (GOT, IT!).

"You see, he is so funny-isn't he Salvo" said Sylvia, as I guess she has been talking about me among her family members but Salvo, did not have last clue, that I have prostetic legs.

Salvo, just looked and took me as I was; my new prosthetic legs worked our well and were hidden from sight-I will break the news with them once I feel more confortable.

"Girls, Mitchell, dinner is on the table" Mother Williams said as she broke the monotony of the two sisters chitter chattering. The mother, the father nor the sister did not notice my legs or either they did not care.

It was an ocward situation. How does one tell the parents of my future wife I was involved in a tragedy early in my life that has had a traumatic affect on me psychologically and physically?

Chapter X

Ubering, More Than Just

A RIDE,

IT'S A SCIENCE.

I could taste and smell the food even before I sat down at the dinner table. My sensory signaled the same way when Sylvia cooks and place the food on the table-delicious. That old southern cooking never fails with the old motto: A Mans Heart Is In His Stomach. So very true from what I can see of the size of Mr. Oscar Alfred Williams, Sylvia's father and the mother just looks so Rosie.

With UBER, I was consistent in my style, for I learned a great deal on how to be polite and courteous to my clients-I took on the qualities and learned them as a science, The UBER Way, treat your client the way you want to be treated. I treated the Williams family the way they treated me and since Mr. Williams had an amputated foot, I guess they all have gone through the ordeal of adjusting from being immobile.

"Army man, yum Mitch" said Mr. Williams, at the dinner table.

"Yes sir-first Calvary, right here in Fort Benning, Georgia Sir" I responded, fast, knowing the next question will probable be how did I get injured during the war; but it was, not.

"Thirty year Marine Corp, Master Sargent-out of Fort Berwick, Louisiana son-those were the days, when we covered the battle fields with feet on the ground instead of Drones in the air" Here goes one of those War stories, I thought to myself, but Mrs. Williams, began to clear the table from the delicious meal and placed the desert of Peach Cobbler Pie, that shut the Old Soldier up, real quick. We ate and then retreated into the Den where we watched football, while the women took to the kitchen too clean and wash the dinner dishes.

"What do you do for a living son?" said Mr. Williams.

"Well Mr. Williams"

"Call me Oscar, Mr. Williams is to formal-just Oscar son"

"Wow, that broke the monotony-he seems like a real gentleman, a career marine man.

"I drive for UBER-Oscar" that felt so ocward, since, calling him Oscar, seemed to me, a sign of friendship, but on the same token, I was having the most incredible sex with his daughter-I tried not to look at Oscar and see the resemblance of the daughter and father. Sylvia, I noticed, had some ways like her father and mother. The daughters in a family usually take on a lot of characteristics as the father and the son take on a lot of characteristics like the mother. Well, anyway, I tried not to say much; I tried to watch the Patriots and the Seattle Game!

"Huber, that's what you said" Oscar was trying to be funny, since I know that Atlanta has UBER drivers.

"No Sir, it's UBER"

"Oh, how is driving for a Taxi Service Son"

"Well, I have driven for UBER for six months and everyday there is another adventure"

"Adventure, what do you mean, adventure son"

"Well, UBER is like a community transportation service, and people within the same areas that you live in, ride UBER-you can talk and find out what is going on in your own neighborhood and have a friendly conversation what is going on in the world"

"It's like that, a barber shop gossip service on wheels-well I be dam-how do you get your passengers son; I mean, do you call the main office or does the main dispatch office call you like The Yellow Cab"

"Cell phone dispatch only, that is how we communicate sir, I mean Oscar"

"The cell phone-that is how you get your passengers"

"Google is the system that UBER uses and it directs the driver, such as me and it tells the passenger where I am as a driver and how long it will take me to get to the pick up place and where to drop off the passenger"

"That is a High Tech system if it can do all of that by just calling into that cell phone"

"It does more than that Oscar, it drives the car I use automatically"

"You don't say-well, I saw that car that drives itself on the news-do you think that it is safe son"

"I drive, well, I mean, I commodore one everyday, since I am with a lost of my legs sir"

"Well, I noticed that son and you lost your legs for the love of your country-my son, he lost his life, not by a injury in the battle field, but by a injury on how people treated him when he returned after serving in the military-Oscar Junior had some deep mental problems after being discharged and there was no help for Junior"

"Yes, I understand sir, it was hard for me also, but I received rehabilitation services and a lot of medical attention, I recovered but a lot of veterans do not" I told Oscar, knowing that he was broken when his son killed himself.

"Come on Mitch, I will show you Oscar's room and the honors he received while in the Core" I got off the coach and we both, hopped up the stairs; Mr. Oscar Williams, with a amputated foot, and I with prosthetic legs and a plastic arm-two war veterans from different era's.

"He opened the door of Oscar Juniors room, and the daughters and his wife did not notice us going into Juniors room-there I saw all the trophies, the pictures and the Marine core flag and the American flag can be overwhelming to look at when a family member has given their life. I could tell that Junior was indoctrinated into The Marine Core keeping up with the Father's footsteps, trying to live in the shoes of his famous Marine Core Father.

"He received many honors and could not live it down when he returned back to the States-he was hyped up, wired up and all he knew is when and how to kill the enemy"

I remained still at a solidary, salute posture, as Mr. Oscar Williams, Senior was overcome by looking at his dead son's pictures and all the honors that his son received, just to be dishonored by the system that he fought for many of years in Iraq and Afghanistan.

Junior, with all his gear on and night goggle's stood in one of the pictures straight up and proud like the American Flag that he fought for that was in the background from the city that his battalion took over in a fierce fight; Iraq, the statue of Sadam Hussein was pulled down by his regiment.

That was quite a feat, pulling down the Statue of Sadam; and now, all that remains of the two are the memories, in pictures visuals of one man's defeat and another man's struggle.

"Mitchell, you better look at the news, one of your UBER buddies being arrested for Molesting a College student" Sylvia, calling me from the bottom of the stairs where I was in her brother's room looking at the mementos and the honors he received.

"Okay, here I come" I stepped down the stairs using the rails, one step at a time while looking at the garage inside door, Mr. Williams must have gone inside the garage to work on his car. He suffered a lot since the suicide of his son and the amputation of his foot. I could tell that losing his son really bothered him.

"Wow, I said to Sylvia, Savoy and Gladys; Sylvia's mothers, when I looked at the news too see a UBER driver arrested for molesting a University of California (USC) college student.

"There is not a day that passes that UBER, is not in the news," I said to The Ladies.

"You drive for UBER Mitch"

"Yes, Soya-been driving for six months for UBER, one of their GOOGLE cars"

"Google car, what kind of a car is that"

"It drives itself and I just commodore the panel by touch screen"

"Mitch sits in the driver seat and sometimes the passenger seat and make sure everything is working okay; the car drives itself, to the Airports and to the local colleges and grocery Market and to the Mall"

"If the cars does all of that Mitch-are you not worried about your job"

All three looked at me for an answer and as I thought about it, they may have a point there, but California will never change the law that a automated car, that self propels driving must not have a body in the seat-the insurance companies will never allow that, or will they"

"Mitch is going into middle management and training the drivers how to operate the UBER cars-so if they ever get rid of the trainers, UBER will be in Hot Water," said Sylvia.

"The old UBER drivers never received any training, you see, the car that UBER driver has is a regular car without the HIGH TECHNOLOGICAL, Google system that allows the car to drive by satellite mode"

"You know a lot about technology don't you Mitch," said Mrs. Williams.

"Well, I try to keep up with the modern technology pertaining to UBER maim-If the driver would have had good training, these incidents would have never happened"

"So you are going to train the new drivers Mitch," said Sonya.

"Yes, it has been confirmed through my cell phone email that I got the position in training the new drivers"

"Why that is great Mitch-I told you you'd get the position" Sylvia, now smiling after hearing the good news that I will be training the new UBER drivers, "hands on", as they learn the Better Qualities of Driving for the public. Always being polite and remembering, The Passenger's Safety Comes First.

It certainly a coincident that as soon as the news broke out about that last UBER driver, accused of a form of molestation. Groping a female is molestation in my book and I will certainly teach and tell the drivers that I train, hands off, for all the passengers and the outside pedestrians.

With a 50 Billion-Dollar Company, what CEO would not invest in a trainer giving up his personal experience and now for Twelve, dollars and Seventy-five cent an hour. It will keep the news media off the executive branch of UBER and training will help the drivers.

"You sure did-so, as soon as we get back, I will start training and I will continue to drive for UBER part time…" Life had changed and UBER made it happen. The freedom of driving, just like when I drove through Europe and then through the Middle East Countries during the wars. The scenery of the structures built thousands of years ago, while on my European tour and the Middle east tour, widened my knowledge and gave me something too strive for. Being able to travel and see how the other people lived in the world was fascinating; so is UBER. I have literally meant people from Italy, Spain, oh, and that place where they give over fifty percent interest on $100,000.00; Switzerland.

"Baby, why where you in juniors room today with Dad" Sylvia asked me while she was getting ready to go to The Underground!

"Well, we talked about the war and the treatment that Junior did not get after he was discharged"

"After he was discharged-Junior was using drugs and getting those drugs from the streets Mitch; so what ever my dad told you, take it with a grain of salt"

""Man, this gal was more classy than I thought; she told me flat out another entirely different story from what her dad told me about Junior not receiving help; Junior, did not want to receive help-that euphoric feeling from smoking that dope was his relief, not getting into a program at The Veterans Hospital, seeing specialist in Mental Health that can help the Veterans get relief from coming out of a tormented war zone.

Sylvia, knew it all…

"Well, have a good time at the Mall" I told Sylvia, as I made sure she had the credit card to purchase what she needed and buy her parents some gifts. Once again, I took a look at what I have been through and what I have now-it is amazing what a job can do, although, it pays little or nothing driving for UBER, It's The Freedom, that you get from driving from community to community, from town to town, from county to county-UBER, offered that freedom, totally, by their Partnership. No benefits, no gas, no maintenance, just freedom in driving….

Chapter XI

The Life of a UBER GROOVER

Never knowing, what the hell is a UBER; is it a synonym of something else? I translated it to be a Manifestation of the new millennium of mobile transportation. While still in Atlanta, I decided to go on Google and find out more about the company in which I have worked for the last six months. Will the company be worthy of me working for the Giant Conglomerate on a manageable basis or will they shunt me as they did before; never answering my emails and as far as the pay, I never received one nickel of the cancelations and the mistakes that I showed up, the passenger cancelled after fifteen minutes and wasted my gas, my time and mileage.

My cell phone rung!

"Yes"

"Mitchell, it's Salvo; Sylvia became ill and we had to take her to Grady Hospital" Oh no, my heart just sunk. The only person that mattered to me in my life, now at the hospital! I got to get a grip on things; I have got to calm down and go to The Grady Hospital.

"What happened, I mean why"

"She was feeling faint and almost fell so we rushed her to the hospital-is she pregnant" Salvo asked.

"She didn't tell you"

"No, I guess she was keeping it a secret but the doctor and mother will know pretty soon"

"Is she in the emergency room"

"Yes, and the family doctor is on her way"

"Okay, I will get your dad to take me to the hospital" I hung up the phone, called out for Mr. Williams and he was already talking to his wife in the garage where he was working on his car. We both took off in his classic fifty-three Chevy since momma Williams had the family car and got to the hospital emergency room in no time.

"Sylvia, are you okay" I asked.

"Yes baby, I am okay, the baby is fine too but the doctor said I got to stay off my feet until the baby gets here"

"Yes baby, anything that will keep you and the baby safe," I told Sylvia.

"We will fix up her old room Mitchell, she can stay with us-she can't take a plane ride, it will harm her and the baby" said Mrs. Williams.

Life has its little un-expectancies at every stop in the road. A little bump here and a pothole there and another one when you think the lights says, go ahead, the light is green-things become red. You got to reb up your engine though and start again. Things become a little smother on the road of life once you get on that clear freeway without traffic.

"No matter what happens, I will be by your side"

"Oh no baby, you got to go back and start your new job as a trainer; you will have study hours and you will not have to drive as much-you will be able to stay home with me and the baby"

"Yeah, I guess you are right, I must go back since I will have a bigger responsibility soon"

"I 'am going to be a grandfather" said Mr. Williams, now at the bedside of his mother to be daughter.

"Yes daddy, you're going to be a grandfather and momma, a grandmother"

"Yes baby, I knew you looked a little plumb and you had that Glow about yourself, did the doctor tell you if it is going to be a boy or girl"

"Mother, I just found out myself and Mitch will keep it a secret until the baby is born"

"Are you having the baby here Sylvia, in Atlanta?" said Salvo.

"I do not know Sister, I just want to rest and be with my husband too be"

"Husband, baby, Lord Have Mercy, everything is happening so fast-why when you all getting married"? Said Mr. Williams.

"Soon, like within the next few days Mr. Williams, before I go back to Los Angeles" I decided for sure right then and there, I could not let the Love of My Life get away from me and she love me so much that she is having my baby.

That Sunday, September 25th. Sylvia Williams and I, Mitchell Justin Martinez was married at her home church. Sylvia, feeling much better now and eating like there was no tomorrow. That Wednesday, I had to board a plane to L. A. and check in with Larry and Carl for The UBER TRAINING PROGRAM.

At The L A X…American Airlines…

"Carl, Larry, how are you two doing"? As they picked me up in one of the new UBER/GOOGLE cars, curve side.

"We are fine Mitch, and we got a lot of work to do; by the way, congratulations on your nuptials" said Larry.

"Yeah Mitch, you see what UBER can do if you just get there" Carl said, what he meant, it was not clear to me, but

I did not even think about it; I missed Sylvia already and I knew, there would be a great adjustment returning to our apartment and not having her there with me.

"Here's what we got Mitch; seven veterans, already qualified and passed the background check-now, here is the itinerary that The Department of Transportation gave us for the guidelines in training these veterans in a two week program to commodore the new UBER/GOOGLE cars"

"What's been changed from the last UBER/GOOGLE cars?" I asked.

"There is a virtual video monitor in the new one's that works like Skype-you can communicate with the driver from the headquarters, at all times with the Wi-Fi application"

"It was approved through the department" I asked, knowing that you have got to get the passengers permission before taping them, taking pictures and using the passengers, their likeness, in any form.

"Yes, we got the same approval as the police have with their body cam"

"The seven veterans, are they war veterans from the Department of Rehabilitation"?

"Yes, some fine guys and gals; all without one or two extremities, ready to drive for UBER/GOOGLE"

"I want to take a look at their portfolio and find out where they have received their medical care and the times of their appointments so it will not conflict with the training"

"Mitch, these guys are recent medical released amputee's from Walter Reed; they have suffered a great deal-they have watched the video's on the new Google driven car application and they watched you commandeering the car-they are all excited about driving"

"Okay Larry, I will do the best I can with the veterans-I have been down that road many times before"

We had lunch at the Santa Monica Grill Restaurant and then went directly to the headquarters of the UBER/GOOGLE site.

"My car, where is it" I asked.

"Right over there Mitch-it has been retro-fitted with the new Skype and all the maintenance that you requested"

"Good" My luggage, from the trip to Atlanta, was placed in the trunk of my car and I went directly to the training center.

Walking into the hanger where the new vehicles were being fitted with the high technical application of: Internet, Wi-Fi, Skype, Blue-Tube and the highest level of video cameras Pro-Cam, that can be installed into a UBER/GOOGLE vehicle.

"For seven drivers, they spent ten million dollars-that makes a lot of sense" I thought to myself, as the trainee's came walking toward me as I took a glance at the new cars.

You're the UBER GROOVER" a vet with a crutch, wearing short pants where I could visibly see the Oscar Petrous leg (Track Runners leg) looked at me, as I looked at him and acknowledging that I picked up the name: UBER GROOVER, since the guys always made jokes that I was "STUCK IN THE EIGHTIES AND NINETIES WITH HIS GROOVE". My cloths, the music I played on my XM oldies radio and some of the things that I said, went way back to the eighties era. I guess I was stuck there, that is where I first enlisted into the Army, so that is where I was Stuck, that is, until I meant Sylvia, my wife.

"You can call me that-UBER GROOVER-that name kind of stuck with me but it will be more appropriate to call me Mr. Martinez while we are in training" I said to the young man whom seemed very well adjusted in his new prosthetic leg. The other six came strolling up to meet me and shake my hand.

"We just want to thank you, for giving us a opportunity to prove ourselves with the new mission that they have given us"

"The federal government and President Obama, made it possible for all of us veterans, I was just the first and now, your trainer" I told the vet, as the other's closed in and just stare at me. I was wearing regular trousers and long sleeve shirt and they could not see my legs.

"Good to meet you fellows and ladies, now, shall we go into the conference room and get started on the mission" As we walked, the most salient question that the disabled veterans asked is: Will They Take Our Disability Pension, Once We Are Trained To Drive?

I told them emphatically NO, they will not, they can not and the law says that they will be in violation of the law if the Disabled Veterans that lost a limb, is at the lost of having their medical and monetary benefits taken from them. That broke the monotony and we got settled in the conference room where I started the classes with the history of UBER and GOOGLE and The Federal Government Program to help The Disabled Veterans and their needs to get gainful employment.

Chapter XII

ℐUBER 101

"This is the class agenda, and these are all the applications; such as Skype, Wi-Fi, Blue Tube, Cell Phone S7 and everything that you were given, as far as the literature to read-DUMP IT, THROUGH IT IN THE TRASH, IT WILL NOT HELP YOU AND IT WILL BE A WASTE OF TIME!"

Telling the five men veterans and the two female veterans what they will need to survive the UBER-STREETS.

"Yeah, that's what I'm talking about," said Charlie, who suffered a facial burn on the right side of his face and was subjected to skin grafting and reconstruction of his eye and nose.

"But, Mr. Martinez, that is what they gave us, this is what we were told to use in case we get in a jam" Cynthia said, as she adjusted her seat to fit her hand, to move closer to the table, shuffling through her papers with her plastic hand.

"I am going to show you, tell you and experience with you, this phenomenon of transporting people at a low cost-besides, all those schematics, diagrams about the equipment installed in your UBER/GOOGLE vehicle, you will never have a chance too look at the contents of those pamphlets, working for UBER"

"Yeah, all man-this guy is for real," said James, the young Black man who suffered the lost of his left foot, not by an IUD, but by a poisonous sand parasite in IRAQ. James took his boots off to wash his cloths and socks after a mission

89

in a water hole full of waste at the bottom and the parasitic worms entered through his socks and his foot and if his foot were not amputated, it would have cost him his life.

"One thing that I must do and that is give you a little background on the company that you are employed by-UBER, founded by…four very intelligent Attorneys and computer savvy young people in San Francisco, with the idea of connecting riders to drivers through the applications of the cell phone, that makes it more accessible, opening up more possibilities for riders and more business for drivers."

"Excuse me Mr. Martinez" Larry, opening the door of the conference classroom while I was giving the new UBER driver their orientation.

"There is just one more trainee that due to the Disability Act, we must admit into the class," I told the drivers to take a few minutes break while I stepped out the door meet driver number 8.

"Mr. Martinez, this is Shamyra, the eight student trainee" I went to shake Shamyra hand and introduce myself and noticed that she wielded a white stick with red at the end with a little round ball at the very end of the stick-oh, Shamyra is Blind, I said to myself.

"How are you Shamyra, my name is Mr. Mitchell Martinez and I am the instructor of the UBER driver" I lend forward, as Shamyra heard me and smiled and put out her hand anticipating for me to take her palm of her hand and give her a courtesy shake, I did, it was strange, but I shook her hand.

"It is a pleasure to meet you Mr. Martinez and I have heard so much about you and the UBER/GOOGLE drivers program" said Shamyra.

I Could tell that she either had an instinctual quality of knowing where I stood as I greeted her or she was not totally blind.

"Come on inside the class Shamyra and meet the other students" As I escorted Shamyra inside the conference room I healed her hand and once I got up to the long conference wooden maple colored table I pulled up a chair, as she knew exactly what to do, she sat down, so gracefully as if she could see and knew everything about her surroundings.

"Class, this is Shamyra Smith and she will be training with us" I told the class and too my surprise, some of the other students knew her while the other students just looked, as to say, with their bottom lip slanted downward, how is she going to drive a UBER/GOOGLE car.

Well, that was yet to be seen, or should I say, heard. The Federal Disability Act prohibits the discrimination of any Veteran for participating in any Federally Funded Program so; we will train Shamira Smith to the best of our ability.

Although the UBER/GOOGLE machines, actually and virtually drives itself, the California Law states that someone has to be inside the drivers seat or the passenger seat at all times. The California Law did not say anything about the Commodore (Assistant Driver) being Blind!

"As I was saying class, the UBER applications are meant for the sole purpose of getting the passengers safely to their destination-what was added over the years was the high technological automatic driving abilities that works by a satellite fifty thousand or more miles in the sky that can see each and everything, from a ant on the pavement where the UBER Mobile must pass through in order to reach the designated trip, to a Diesel truck driving in the front, in the back and on the side of a UBER MOBILE"

"Wow, they must have spent a lot of money to make a car drive on it's own Mr. Martinez" said Brian, a veteran that lost both of his arms and like myself, had plastic arms that he used mechanically, driven by sensors from the brain to distinguish touch and to grabs objects.

My maternal instincts were kicking in while training these 21, 22 and 23 year old kids; they are just babies, knowing nothing of how the world evolves or how the economy works. More than likely, these eight veterans signed up to go fight in the war, not even knowing the consequences. The eight were from different diversified backgrounds, White, Black, Oriental, Hispanic and Male and Female. They painted a clear picture of America and the need and willingness to Work and keep things moving no matter what happened in the past. I had the responsibility to guide these eight student trainee's to a path that will determine their entire life's of the work ethic, and training them too be productive citizens no matter what the circumstances were in their past. I was to become a father, so I bonded with these students and my job is too keep them out of Harms Way!

After giving the eight trainees' their initial orientation, Lunch was catered, right inside the hanger and the new student drivers ate pizza and drunk pepsi and coke beverages. They all went through a lot in their young life's and I noticed how they all went out of there way to talk to one another and help one another, knowing, that they all have gone through the Vocational Rehabilitation Program-they helped each other as if they were siblings-There was a clear Veterans Bond between the eight and myself.

After lunch, the unveiling of the new UBER/GOOGLE retrofitted computerized transportation vehicle was to take place at the UBER/GOOGLE Headquarters in Santa Monica. Once served as a airport, the old Santa Monica airport became to small for the airfield and the residence complain about aircraft crashes such as the crash of the actor Harrison Ford and his vintage plane. Three hangers were purchased by UBER/GOOGLE to modify the vehicles to meet the needs of the drivers and the riders with the computerized electronics.

"Future UBER drivers, here it is, the new UBER-MOBILE" Larry and Carl pulled the curtain, and it was just like I imagined, a SRX, Cadillac with the large dome on top to input the activities from the satellite and the UBER colors of the sign; quite impressive, as I explained the new vehicle too Shymira and she, once Larry and Carl explained the capabilities of the BILLION DOLLAR VEHICLE, Shymara, went up too the car and felt the contour from the front of the vehicle to the rear and she gave us a graphic description on what she was feeling even the color of the car, the aero-dynamics of the shape of the SUV and the bubble top dome where electron data is received and guides the vehicle to it's destination. It was a modern technical dream of the scientist that designed this vehicle and The Future Mode of transportation.

Class for today was complete, as the eight students, waiting for their van to take them to their dorms at The Veterans Medical Center, Brentwood, asked more and more questions. They were so excited that they were chosen to break the mode in transporting people into the new millennium of travel…

Chapter XIII

Mobility

Just as the UBER fleet is always mobile, so will the eight drivers be. Day three of the training is where I let the driver, one by one, take the wheel and become mobile. From the months that most of the veterans went through their rehabilitation, in which most of them were medevac from Afghanistan, too Wiesbaden Military Hospital where they received surgery from their wounds; then Walter Reed Medical Hospital near Washington, D.C. where multiple surgeries and the healing process occurred. They remained immobile for months at a time, that is, until they were fitted and the designers made them new legs and arms. An adjustment, physically and psychologically was in the processes of getting these veterans back to their goals in life and my job was the final stage in getting the Veterans Mobile and able to live Independently.

"Let the system work for you Brian, you do not have to touch the screen or talk to the voice function until you're given the okay to start"

"But Mr. Martinez, I just want to turn on The Heat radio station and hear some beats"

"Some Beats, you'll hear the beats when a Diesel Truck comes side swiping you on the road; now calm down and get started before turning on the XM radio"

"Okay, Mr. Martinez"

"Now, since the signal has picked up your destination and you have confirmed your trip, you can turn on the radio, but not load, I got to hear and see what you are doing from the back seat"

"Yes Sir" said Brian, a young kid that is into hip-hop and rap. Brian would often take his wheelchair and Dance of Wheels, where he maneuvered the Wheel Chair to Dance Hip Hop with the wheels, twilling and moving the wheel chair back and forth in sync with the music. Without legs, the wheel chair was his mobility when he took off his prosthetic apparatus. It was a real sight to see how he Danced with The Wheel Chair.

"Now that you have your destination, accept or reject by talking to the voice command Brian"

"Accept" said Brian, as the UBER/GOOGLE vehicle rolled out of the gates.

"It will take you twenty-two minutes to arrive at your location," said the Google application, while Brain, tickled pink, that he was actually at the realm of the latest mode of transportation ever created.

Even smoother than I could ever imagine. The technology used in this UBER Mobile tops The Beast, used by the President. This vehicle has tracking, blue tube, Wi-Fi, just three functions that the president's vehicle does not have due to tracking his vehicle and signaling a destructive mode. The seven UBER SRX's is estimated to make hundreds of thousands of dollars in just one week. A twenty four hour, seven days a week, UBER has expanded it's travel log to pick up at the airports, drive passengers from San Diego to San Francisco and Las Vegas, Nevada with a special permit to enter, but no pick up's in Las Vegas due to insurance issues.

"Brian, you have arrived at your destination-your client has been notified" said the app.

"There's Larry and Carl standing at gateway 4, the vehicle will attaché to Larry's cell phone and pull over to the curb automatically Brian"

"You mean I don't have to do anything"

"No, all you do is just sit in the driver's seat or the passenger's seat and enjoy your trip"

"This is boring"

"Boring-why what did you think you were going to do Brian-your job is just like a door man, all you got to do is press the button on the dash where is says P-L, passenger's door, left side and the door will automatically open too let your passenger inside your cab; like a door man at The Hilton" I explained to Brian and thought to myself, maybe I should have required that they read all the manual's and the pamphlets.

A task that a three year old can do, but what else can a double amputee do to make a living? Brain and the three other amputees' could not be a doorman; there legs will ware out standing all day. This is the idea job for them to do being that they are not even required to get out of their vehicle – boring yes, innovative yes, inspiring no!

"Brian, Mitch-I sees that all the training has paid off, Brian and four of the other's are just about ready to take a independent mission"

"Yes, they are ready, but what about Shamira Smith, she may not be able to handle all of this-you know people can be very rude at the airports and on the 405 freeway toward other drivers-how are they to know that she is blind, even though the car is driven by satellite"

"We have just the place for Mrs. Smith, she will work with her team of drivers that she has trained with, on the

Skype Monitors and communicate with the other drivers at her own convenience by using the application: Dragon, Naturally Speaking on the GOOGLE satellite system"

"How does that work"?

"You speck into the mica, like the one that is placed inside the vehicles of our SRX's and Mrs. Smith will receive the messages from her colleagues and respond," said Larry.

"If the other driver gets in a jam at three o'clock in the morning transporting a passenger to the airport, Mrs. Smith will guide them through the applications"

"That is an excellent idea-do you think that Mrs. Smith will accept the new position"

"She is the type of a person that will work with the project in any way she can to complete the mission" Larry, Carl and I agreed, that putting Shymara Smith, the Blind veteran will be too strenuous and subject her to unduly stress and strain while she can work with the UBER/GOOGLE communications with Skype to talk to the driver's and keep them company while no passengers are inside their vehicle.

Back at the Headquarters…

"Shymaray, we all know that you wanted to assist in driving the UBER vehicle's but the way things stand now; it will be virtually impossible due to the climate of the crowded freeways and airports" I was straight up with Mrs. Smith.

"So, all this training I received was just for nothing" She said, as she took off her dark glasses to rub her eyes and hold back the tears.

"We are placing you in the front office of the headquarters to monitor the drivers that are having problems with the clients and with their vehicles"

"Really, why that will be nice; you mean to tell me that I will be in The UBER Simulator and monitoring the drivers with their problems-why it will be just like driving a UBER/ GOOGLE vehicle"

"Yes, that is the whole idea and you will be working with the mechanics, the engineers and the technicians that designed the cars"

"Oh, thank you Mr. Martinez; I always knew that there will be something else for me to do in my life when I became 100% blind during the war; now, I can work in the UBER Simulator and be a Damage Control coordinator-that is great" Shymara Smith, was very pleased with her new position and the coordinator actually paid more money than the drivers on a salary basis. It was good to have one of my students satisfied on taking an indirect position with UBER; after all, she sacrificed

Her life for the freedom of the country and she deserved to have something of the American Dream…

Now, I must prepare the other seven drivers' their certificate of training

With the UBER 101 classes they have completed. Everything must be documented and recorded since the Federal Government will audit the books and all the expenses, that amounted to Six Million Dollars, in salaries, technology, the purchase of the SRX Cadillac, all seven, and the lodging/meals for a staff of sixty technicians and mechanics. That was the estimates for only one month of the program. If they plan on recruiting more drivers it may cost Ten Million Dollars a month.

All seven driver became mobile and took on their task of transporting business clients, vacation people, tourist to amusement parks, but we had to exclude the door to door pick up due to the neighborhoods narrow streets and the GOOGLE Maps misreading the correct addresses. Due to The Upcoming El Nino', the rain fall of the century, several roads were closed and the

UBER/GOOGLE vehicles were stuck in traffic because the technicians were not notified of the Road Closures.

The mobility program worked out so well that the trucking industry and the bus transportation services wants to employ the same technology, but what price must be paid for the technology vs. the employment of personal. Whenever there is money to be saved and the compensation of not paying workman's compensation and medical benefits, owners and Chief Executive Officers are going to jump on the opportunity to save money, make more money and increase their mobility.

The seven students, that suffered physical and psychological damages from a senseless war, now were mobile once again and enjoying there UBER/GOOGLE jobs.

Chapter XIV

UBER Compensation

Back in Atlanta for a week, enjoying my wife and her family, as Sylvia gained a tremendous amount of weight. I went to the doctor with her and there were two heartbeats; that meant twins. I knew that when I did have sex, it was going to be a 'Wang-Bagger', but I never imagined that I would be having twins. We kept the gender secret but the notice that we are having twins spread like wild fire in the entire Williams Family. All things were just wonderful on the home front, that is, until I started receiving calls from my former trainee's.

"Mr. Martinez" A call came in directly to my cell phone while I was watching the football game in the Den of The Williams Home.

Yes, this is Mr Martinez.

"This is Brian Steinke, and I just received a letter from the Department of the Treasury telling me that they will be reducing my monthly compensation from 100% to 70% because I am gainfully employed by UBER now"

"There must be a mistake Brian, have you called the Department of Veterans Affairs Office" I asked Brian, who is a double amputee from the war and only working part time for UBER while he continued receiving medical attention for the wounds that he suffered during the war. For the government to take thirty present of his benefits will mean that he must work full time in order to pay for his housing and food.

"There must be a mistake Brian, since the Uber Company and Rehabilatation Services informed me they will not take the disabled veterans disability payments".

"James, you called and left a message-I was talking to Brian while you called, how are things going"? I called James Malone, the UBER/GOOGLE driver that I trained a few months ago. James was part of the program to get the Amputee veterans back in the workforce like Brian.

"Mr. Martinez, can you do something, they send me a letter to notify me that my Social Security Disability check will stop next month-well, I have three kids and we just moved into a home, big enough for my wife, my Children and my mother in law-I can not afford to live here with just a UBER part time job" He was almost in tears for the mere fact that James and the others were deceived. Once they started working, the federal government listed them employed and their disability was stopped. For a local trip, a driver, Making six dollars and three dollars and eighty-seven cent for a trip with a passenger in a pool just does not pay the rent in Los Angeles. I got to call Larry, the director of the new UBER/GOOGLE training program and plead with him that the drivers should go on a salary instead of being paid one dollar per mile and eighteen cent per minute.

"Larry, how are you," I said.

"Mitchell, how are things in Atlanta" Larry responded.

"Oh, just fine, but things are really getting ugly in Los Angeles, aren't they"

"Well, what do you mean Mitch"?

"Three of the UBER/GOOGLE drivers; I just spoke to them and they told me that their disability checks are being cut altogether and some disabled Vets pensions are being cut Thirty or more percent" I was hot under the collar.

"Yeah Mitchell, that is what I have been hearing-you see, we tried too fight for the veterans but congress and the senate informed us that the whole idea of having a rehabilitation program is to get the veterans back on their feet"

"Back on their feet, Larry, five of the disabled veterans legs were blown off in Afghanistan and Iraq, what do you mean back on their feet-they sacrificed their lives Larry and now the Federal Government with the Plan that UBER made to rehabilitate the disabled veterans; well they were thrown under the bus, or should I say, under their Armored Tank again" I was pissed by now. Getting it from the horse's mouth, that this was all in the plan with The UBER and The Feds.

"They will reject it Larry, they will surely form UNIONS and reject the whole Plan, just you wait and see-they think that they are saving millions of dollars in tax payers money and UBER and GOOGLE are getting Tax incentives but one thing you do not mess with and that is THE VETERANS….

"There's nothing we can do, it has already been signed through the senate and the congress and UBER is not going to give the drivers any more money-do you realize that UBER and GOOGLE has invested over Five BILLION DOLLARS on The Project"

"How much did they squeeze the palms of your hands with Larry " You see, I read the books and did the accounting work and Larry, Carl and the rest of his crew were getting money from the federal government illegally.

Soon as I get back to Los Angeles, I will have a meeting with the UNIONS and voice my rejection of the UBER

DRIVERS, from all over the WORLD, being treated like a HUMAN SWEAT SHOP on WHEELS with three and four dollars on the average for a ride. The poor veterans, their prosthetics legs are being wore and swelling because they will have to work double time and drive triple time just to make ends meet. As for the regular drivers; Lord Knows how they are getting by…

When they tell you, it is too good to be true, believe them! UBER would not change their Partner business with the drivers; the federal Government would not change their disability definition of employability and employability. That decision reduced the pensions payments by Eight Hundred and Fifty Dollars per month, to over seven thousand veterans; people living off general relief received nothing; college students financial aid was reduced and penalties were sent to pay the over payments of being paid while working for UBER while at the same time, claiming no income on their financial aid statements. UBER has changed the entire financial transportation system.

"Mitch, you can't fight a multi billion dollar business like UBER, why you're in jeopardy of losing your job and you have a family too support," said Sylvia.

"Son, I would not mess around with those Indians, you see what happened when they took over India with Six Billion people; that Gandhi fellow said Turn the other cheek and those English ran-just think what they will do to a Black man" said Mr. Williams.

"The owner of UBER is an American Dad, not India; he is from India descent, that's" as I tried to correct my father in-law.

"Didn't UBER give you a new start in your life Mitchell, why if it were not for UBER, you would not have meant my sister" said Salvo.

"Well, just let Mitch do what he got to do, besides, just think what would have happened if Martin Luther King would have said, well, that's okay, soon or a later, the minorities, the women, the gays will get their equal rights-where would we be today if he would not have acted to make a change in our system" said Mrs. Williams, and they were all right; UBER did lift me from a life of destitute, while at the same time, my net worth changed but the Federal government could never take my pension because I spent twenty years at The Veterans Hospital and my pension is vested- One half of the members in Congress and the Senate receive the same Military Disability Pension, so why would they vote on a bill that would take their owe salary?

My wife, my sister in law and my father in law gave me their opinion what I should do. I took all of there suggestions into consideration and decided to be incognito; that is, I will write the Department of Transportation and the other Federal Organizations and express to them how unfair it is for the Federal Government to take the disabled veterans disability and the other welfare recipients funds on a bogus accounts of The UBER Partner's. After all, I am The UBER-GROOVER!

Chapter XV

UBER-GROOVER

ACCOUNTABILITY

My wife, sister-in-law, and father-in-law gave me their opinions on what I should do. I took all of their suggestions into consideration and decided to go incognito; that is, I would write the Department of Transportation and the other federal organizations, and express to them how unfair it is for the Federal Government to take the disabled veterans' disability and the other welfare recipients' funds, to use on a bogus account of The UBER Partner's.

The Department of Transportation, never responded; The Department of Vocational Rehabilitation for Veterans, never compensated the disabled veterans for their wartime injuries and driving for UBER. Just as people were so gullible with all the hype of a Weapon of Mass Destruction, during the Iraq war, so was congress and the senate sold on UBER. UBER, a transportation company that makes $50,000,000,000 Fifty Billion Dollars, can not afford to pay it's driver an extra three hundred dollars a month? Where are those CEO's morals, where is those executives accountability. Where is Justice?

"Mitch, Mitchell Martinez, we want to see you at the headquarters of UBER today" It was Larry, the once director, now promoted to a managerial position. I knew that there would be trouble once they find out that I was writing the federal government complaining. Well, I was two steps ahead of them, since I had already copied all the files and the

Fiscal accounts of the payouts and the funds from the federal government that was suppose to go toward the training and equipment for the UBER/GOOGLE program for veterans, and the underprivileged.

"I am on my way Larry, I am in the area, at the LAX and as soon as I make my drop off I will be right there" I told Larry, and gave a command to the UBER system to go directly to the Headquarters in Santa Monica.

Sepulveda Avenue did not look the same as I looked at the people who were once glad, happy that they were given a brake in their door-to-door transportation arrangements from the sweating backs and the agony and defeat of the UBER drivers. The streets had a whole new meaning, since, the passengers, never, ever once complain about taking a four dollar ride in a brand new Malibu car to the market, to school and to work. It was just the drivers that did not get the free lunch; as we all know: There is no such thing as a free Lunch, in economics 101. UBER 101, had took on a new meaning-exploit one economically deprived group and "PIT" them against the other group and let them fight for the scrapes of the bread left over for that day.

That very street, when I first began my UBER driving is where I took an elderly lady to the market and then I took her back home only to discover that she had locked her keys inside her house. Right here, on Palms avenue and Sepulveda, I waited, right here, for the locksmith as Mrs. Shultz's waited, with her groceries inside my car until the locksmith arrived. It must have taken hours, but I was more than a UBER driver, I was a citizen on a mission to help those that have suffered the burden of being elderly, disabled and unwitting. I was on a mission to safe humanity at the time. Mrs. Shultz's got into her house where her cats eagerly waited for her, as I helped her unload her groceries. She gave me a ten-dollar tip and I refused, but I in turn, gave the money to the Paralyzed Veterans of America; that was before I got married.

"Hello Larry-our should I say, executive Larry" I greeted Larry and Carl was there sitting down ready to give me the bad news.

"Mitch, how could you do such a thing as to writing the department of transportation and rehabilitation telling them that the disabled veterans and the welfare people that we trained are being exploited by UBER"?

"They are Larry-anytime that a driver works for ten hours and only makes Twenty-Seven Dollars for the entire day, that is being exploited financially by their employer" I told Larry, as Carl, taking notes, edged up in his seat.

"The people we trained Mitch, why they love their jobs driving for UBER, why they are able to call it a day, anytime they choose and they are able to go down to their welfare office and get their food stamps and general relief funds, just by making the command: All Systems Down-now how can you beat a job like that"

"Beat, a job like that; Larry, the reason they go to the welfare office, in case you had not thought about it, is because they only made a few dollars that week and need money to feed their children-the reason they go to their doctors appointments is because they complain to their physicians and welfare workers too put them back on warfare since UBER is not paying them any money-can't you see that Larry"? I broke it down to Larry and Carl.

"You could have expressed those problems with us Mitchell, instead of going to the Federal Government; why were you trying to get us defunded" said Carl, now the director in charge of training.

"Yes, I did everything in the book to get those funds that the Federal Government allocated to the underprivileged back into their pockets-you received Billions of Dollars Carl, Larry and what did you people do, squandered the funds by paying off those congressmen and senators; well you can't pay off me" I said, and the two just looked at me and gave me a termination letter, commencing immediately.

"What is this Larry, Carl" Knowing full well what it was, I just looked into there faces, since they were my friends for the last nine months as we started a remarkable program, that was suppose to help the underprivileged people.

"You have been terminated Mitchell" said Larry.

"Terminated, why I am a Partner, you will have to go to the Board to terminate me-I am a UBER Partner, that is what UBER calls it, I own part of the UBER business, I pay for my own gas; I got to pay for my own maintenance; I am a business partner and I got to pay for my own equipment-I am a Partner with UBER" Me, yelling at Larry and Carl at this time.

"The car is yours, but the equipment is ours' Mitch, sorry"

"Oh no, I paid for everything inside and out of that car, that is my BU' and you will have to get passed me to get anything out of that car"

"Very well-Carl, hit the unlock system to the Malibu and retrieve our GOOGLE system and electronics"

"IT, it will not work," said Carl, as he kept pressing the button and trying to enter my Malibu too snatch out the cell phone, the GOOGLE Command system and the rest of the equipment, which would have disabled my vehicle.

"Do you think for one minute that I would leave you two monsters with the keys to my car-so you could come and take it and leave me helpless-those locks and electronics were changed months ago, knowing what you two are capable of doing-you savages" I strutted out of the hanger and hit the command button to my BU' and got inside the car as Larry and Carl kept tainting me to stop and give them their equipment as I just drove off the premises and went straight to Norwalk to retain an attorney to prevent Larry, Carl and UBER from tearing my system apart to get the remaining electronic devises from the vehicle. I set the command for Bu' to take me to Downey to the Chop Shop and have that tracking devise taken out of BU' the car I legally owned and had the pink slip too but all the formalities and legal documents would have me turn in the car.

"Mr. Martinez, we heard what happened with you trying to help us; is everything okay now" said Brian, the UBER driver I trained.

"Yes, now it is, everything is great, why my attorney is drawing up the documents to file a Class Action Law Suit against UBER/GOOGLE for all the money that is owed to the drivers" I told Brian.

"We can't do anything else but drive for UBER now Mr. Martinez, since they have already taken our disability" "Yes, I know but with a good defense, and all the documents on how the funding was misallocated, we have a good case"

"Wow, you use those big words and I am sure everything will work out for us in the long run"

"Speaking of run, how has things been with your driving Brian"

"Slow, real slow-it seems like things would have picked up this time of year but since all those articles written in the Times Newspapers about UBER, it seems, that the people are behind us, the same people that got dam near a free ride with us, well, they stopped ordering UBER and now they take Lyth"

'The Times newspaper has an article on our fight for benefits and a salary increase"?

"Yeah, oh, that's right, you were in Atlanta and did not get your regular news paper-the times newspaper is doing a follow-up on The UBER and the paper has got the attention of the people that use UBER"

"There accountability will be shot down-I will go to the Times newspaper and talk to them this afternoon- oh, and thank you Brian for keeping me informed" Brian, a True UBER-Grover, now, a Grover Mover.

Chapter XVI

Grover's and Mover's!

With over 1000 passengers that I have had the pleasure of taking to the airport, the banks, the grocery stores and to college, my UBERING Days were done…the news of my termination was so greatly exasperated. I would see some of my former passengers at the post office or the market and they would tell me their personal stories of the UBER drivers that they encountered and how my termination went from absconding (Stealing) the monthly payroll; to me running a Chop Shop with stolen UBER vehicles.

"Mitchell, you know I had a UBER driver that had his grandchildren in the back of the car seat" said Mrs. Littlefield, a local passenger that lived in Long Beach that I drove to her job at the bakery in the mornings.

"Really-well it takes all kinds doesn't it Mrs. Littlefield"

"We miss you and how polite you were toward your people Mitchell-here, this is a few dollars to hold you over until you start driving again" Mrs. Littlefield gave me five dollars and I gladly accepted it.

The tales of a UBER driver, with a five star rating and almost 1000 passengers. I could write a book on my experiences-for a matter of fact, that is what I will do; write a book about Grooving and Moving in a UBER Mobile. No, no one would believe those stories, or will they. The Times newspapers could not believe me, that is, until I showed them the records of my driving. All the clients that I waited at their door for fifteen to a half an hour only to find out that they had cancelled their trip but I was never notified and never paid for my gas and time.

"Mitchell, well how and the heck have you been man" a gentleman that got my attention at the Department of Motor Vehicle said.

"Oh hi-" I remembered him; he was the man that got his car stolen, his truck, at the seven eleven store while he was getting some coffee-well we went all over the city looking for his truck that day and almost found it when we were notified that his credit card was in the process of being used in Bellflower-we just missed the perpetrators and I felt really bad that the thief's got away with his golf clubs and other valuables.

"I got my truck back Mitchell, but I did not get my golf clubs; say, I really appreciate you helping me track down those thieves" Steven, was his name, I remembered.

"Mitchell, if you need a job, just look me up; I am retired now but my son runs the welding business-I heard what happened to you working for UBER"

"You did-oh my, the entire Long Beach area and Seal Beach, knows about what happened-well thank you Steven, I will consider your offer"

Wow, everywhere I went, there were people that recognized me as The UBER driver. That was an indication to me that I must have been doing a good job.

With Sylvia, having the babies any day now, I got to find a job-all I can possibly do is, I have been paid to do, that's driving. I applied to DAV-EL and Chuck Limousine Services (CLS) two of the biggest companies in the nation. I got an interview.

"So you worked for UBER," said the vice president of CLS.

"Yes, I drove for UBER for an entire year" I responded to Sidney, the vice president of the western regional transportation for CLS.

"We heard all about you, and how you were the first too start the UBER/GOOGLE search cars, the one's that automatically drove themselves, with the assistance of a commodore, which is required by law of course"

"Yes sir Mr. Whitfield"

"Just call me Sidney-and, if you still are looking for a position at CLS, you can start when ever you are available" Sidney said.

"Well thank you, but Sidney, you said that there is a position, not just a driving job, did I miss something"?

"Oh no, of course you will be able to drive occasionally, but the multi-million dollar company of CLS, needs your skills to update their systems, just like you did for UBER" Oh boy, this was the greatest interview that I ever had-they hired me with no questions asked, just on the note that people talk and CLS listened. With a Five Star rating from UBER, how could I go wrong?

With over one hundred thousand limousines all throughout the country and Europe CLS is an international company that wanted to use the UBER technology to track their drivers.

"Here is your office, right here in one of our trailers-we establish all of our offices near the airport which makes it convenient for us to pick up A-Listers" said Sidney.

"Great idea, but the technology that I suggest you use will not be necessary to pay the high lease on this high bid rent curve area-why the airport, this is the highest rentals in the entire city of Los Angeles" "Do you have another area that we can park our fleet of Limousines and have access to the airport traffic Mr. Mitchell Martinez"

"The Long Beach Pier, why you can pay less than your paying here for these prime lease area's and you can safe a substantial amount-the computer program will let you know exactly how many sedans, limousines, buses and if you need bring in one of your boats; it is all done by programming the computer by satellite" I just gave Sidney little pieces of the information about what I knew from working with UBER. All of UBERS technology was at my exposal; I copied their Major Manifestation to Control The World's Total Transportation Modem.

"CLS, was a major Mover and Shaker throughout the entire world but when the company split due to the divorce of our CEO, Chuck; we took a close second with DAV-EL, now, we are all at a lost with that new UBER/GOOGLE technology-what is it anyway"

"What is what"

"What is UBER"?

"You don't know, Sidney"

"All we know is that once, we saw just a few UBER cars dropping off passengers than there were a few more and more, than, it became a phenomenon-what the hell is UBER anyway, how do they do it"?

"Exploit"

"Ex-who" said Sidney.

"UBER, uses the old techniques of Dividing and Conquering-that's an Exploitive mode that, according to economics, Buy Low, Sell High"

"Buy low, sell High-why we are not selling any thing, we transport people"

"People are a commodity that move from one point to another; now, those people must be transported to do business, to go home to go to school, you name it, they must reach their destination, like apple's and oranges on a semi truck, they must be moved, for a handsome price off course"

"Well Mr. Martinez, we are not moving apple's and oranges to where houses, we are moving people-there is a big difference"

"No difference to UBER, you see, UBER takes the drivers and brain wash them into thinking that they are doing a great service for people in their own community, but the bottom line, UBER offers gas cards that only have 10% of a discount, they offer Five Stars that ultimately brings the race between the driver even close to the finish line, but the only one that finishes is the one with the $50,000,000,000 Billion Dollars-that's the UBER Executives" I told Sidney the entire Code of the success of UBER; The Exploitation of the drivers; with no benefits, no fuel and no future….

After a few weeks past!…. "Mitchell, with your technological knowledge, you have increased the mobility of CLS three times the regular dispatch. Now tell me, how did you do it?"

"All ten thousand limousine drivers have a smart phone now; it was required with the new apps, Chuck Jr. (CLS). You see, with UBER, timing is everything now. When you can get the fleet moving, you have that open window of vehicles coming into the dispatch, refueling and taking breaks, and the time it takes to pick up and drop off a client—all the timing is set by a Google Maps' computer through the World Timing Synchronization Application."

"You mean to tell me that the limousine drivers get a notification on their new smart phones and they rush into the dispatch offices and get their assignment, fuel up, and then they're on their way to the pick up?"

"Even easier than that. They are already fueled up and they have their clients already on their smart phone, tracking them and the client, on the client's cell phone, and the client is tracking the limousine driver. You save time and money."

"Oh boy, you are a genius, Mitchell."

"No, it was not me, it was UBER and those UBER geeks," I said sadly, since I did miss the chase of the UBER game—the timing to get to an assignment, observe, then carry out the mission. This is the way that I was taught, since the military and I only applied those techniques when I first started UBER.

"Mitchell, what's wrong? Why, you have done a fantastic job in the last few months for our company, and received a bonus for changing our old system into the new system. Is there anything I can help you with?" asked, the President of CLS, Chuck Jr. (CLS).

"I would like to go back to Atlanta and be with my wife; she is expecting to deliver any day now."

"That's all? That's it? Well, why didn't you say something? I will have my executive driver take you to the airport and arrange for you to be picked up at the Atlanta gateway."

"Why, thank you, Chuck Jr, but the traffic is bad this time of day on the 405 freeway."

"We are flying you out on one of our private Lear jets, compliments of our company. You will be going out of the Burbank Airport, Mercury Terminal II. Now, do you have any clothes packed?"

"Yes, Sir. A soldier is always ready. I have a bag in the trunk of my car just in case I would have been scheduled to make that Las Vegas run, Sir."

What an amazing guy that Chuck Jr. was, letting me use the company limousine and company Lear jet. On top of that, a holiday bonus! No matter how much I miss UBER, I could never get these kinds of perks from driving with another well established transportation company, I have a family to support now, so here I go . . . to Atlanta.

Chapter XVII

Arrival Time: 11:05 p.m.

The Atlanta limousine driver drove me straight to the William's home.

"That's an UBER car. Well I mean, darn, that company sure has gotten big, Mitchell."

"No, Pops, this is a private limousine company that I work for now. They arranged for me to fly to Atlanta in their private jet and take a limousine to your house from the airport."

"Now that is what I call service. Do you mind if I just sit inside the limousine, Son?"

"Sure, Dad, go ahead. The driver says it's okay. Have a drink; it's on the company's tab now.

How is Sylvia? I asked.

"As big as she can get, Son. Whoa! You sure know how to pack them in, Son.

"Excuse me, Mr. Williams."

"Oh, I had to open my mouth! Go on inside, Son. Sylvia and the women are expecting you, and the door is open."

"Okay." As I walked inside the home of the Williams' there was my baby. "Wow, she has gained a lot of weight since the last time I saw her."

"Honey, you look so prescious. I really missed you."

"I missed you too, Darling, and I want to go home."

"Yes, I know, and as soon as the babies arrive we will go back to Los Angeles on the private company jet."

"Babies, Mitch. I just wanted to tell you—not one, not two, but three babies. The doctor confirmed it. One of the babies had the same timing the heart beat and there are three babies."

"Sylvia, so Rosie and . . . plumb—oh boy, I got to do some overtime now . . . ."

"How's your new job, I mean position, Mitch?"

"They gave me a bonus and flew me all the way here in their private jet," I told my wife, who knew me and looked at me and felt there was something wrong.

"You're not happy with your new position, are you Mitch?" she asked as she got up off the couch like a newborn filly, holding her legs steady, crippling, struggling, until I helped her up.

"I miss the run, the split decisions in the road, forming my own decisions on who I should grant the privilege of riding with the UBER GROOVER, King."

"The what, Mitch? Did you say you're the UBER GROOVER, King? Are you having withdrawals of driving UBER?" Sylvia asked, as she held her belly. She was due any minute now.

"Everywhere I go, my old passengers recognize me, like Mamma Stone whom I saved the day her son, Sam, got into an argument with her when Mamma was going to her doctor's appointment. Sam cancelled the entire trip, on his cell phone. If I hadn't heard the conversation, I would not have believed it! I paid for Mamma Stone's trip and gave her some money to buy lunch and catch a bus back home from Memorial Hospital."

"Mitch, you have done some nice things for the hundreds of passengers that you made life a little easier for in their travels and in their pocketbook, but look at me—you're getting three more passengers to tote around. You have got to get them to their destination—college—in eighteen years of travel time."

Oh, so witty! That southern touch, that's why I love her and will keep that high paying job, and take care of my family,

"Oh, oh! Did you go on the floor?" I asked Sylvia, as I could see water spouting on the hardwood floor like a windshield wiper spraying a mist on the glass.

"My water! My water broke! It's time, Mitchell. It's time to go to the hospital!"

"Okay, Honey. I will get the car. Oh boy, your dad took a ride in the limousine and he has the keys to your parents' car!"

"Momma, it's time"

"What was that baby" mother Williams trembling down the stairs to see what her expected daughter was yelling about.

"Momma, her water broke, and dad has the keys to the car"

"Oh my. Oh my; well, look here Mitch, there is another key hanging inside the garage, right on the right; on the rack-I will get her bag and you pull the car out of the garage"

"Okay momma; I will drive the car out and then come to the front door and get Sylvia, load her inside the car and then we will be off to the hospital"

"Hurry up Mitch-she is already dilating, those three babies want to see their daddy, momma and grandparents now, they aren't going to wait, hurry Mitch"

"Okay" Wow, I never drove any body to the hospital to have a baby-in all my UBER days, I aren't never drove no mother's to the hospital-what do I do now"?

"Hurry Mitch" I heard them calling me and while pop's was taking a spin in the limo, I was starting up his car and taking it out of the garage and Mrs. Williams and I finally got Sylvia inside the car"

"Oh Hurry Mitch" said Sylvia.

"Okay, I will put my GOOGLE MAPS on to get the shortest route, there we are, we are going right toward the hospital; Grady Hospital; oh no, we forgot your mother, I thought that she was in the back seat with you"

"Keep driving Mitch, mother is going to wait for dad and Sonya will be at the hospital probably before we get there"

Oh, I am glad that you rehearsed this, I am sorry honey but it has been a long time since I have driven a regular car but I got this hot rod going, there is the hospital now-look, the nurses are expecting us, the gurney is already in the front-we made it" Wow, what a drive, it was a good thing that GOOGLE gave me the right directions; I would have never made it on time if not. They wheel her into the delivery room of the hospital and her doctor arrived and the other assistant doctors were on hand. I robbed up and had a problem tying the, rope to the back of my gown that the nursing staff gave me; Sylvia was in a lot of pain, I held her hand and practice breathing techniques; then, knowing that the breathing techniques were not working I talked and talked to Sylvia and gave her a pictorial description of a drive up the Pacific Coast Highway, a drive, that we often took in our courting days.

Look, no hands; as I remembered telling Sylvia, as GOOGLE MAPS automatic vehicle drove itself down the Pacific Coast Highway:

The ocean smell like fresh Chrisatemen during Christmas as we glance at the sea with it's brilliant blues and aqua brilliance divides itself as the water pounds on the sea shore; relentless to all those who cross it's path…

I continued to serenade Sylvia by talking and talking to her, calming her down and her mother and Mr. Williams arrived and her sister, at her side kept pampering Sylvia as she was about to give The Breath of Life to three babies.

"Here is your first son" Wow, he came out real feisty, fighting like a feather weight; just a moving and kicking his legs-his legs was one of the first thing I was clued into seeing, just thinking that maybe, he would have abnormality, although, my legs were "Blown Off" with my left arm-not hereditary, not a genetic deficiency, just evil minded beaucracy and politics as usual.

A UBER POOL, three little riders, the boy first, kicking and as strong as a lion, then a little girl, a little less of a fighter, but I could tell, she will rule the boys; she will be the leader, the voice, their commander; then, already sucking his thumb, the little boy came; quite and just breathing on his own but the nurses still took the precautions in putting the babies in a incubator, after cleaning the three up.

"Mitch, did you ever think that you would have three little one's, all at the same time" said Momma Williams.

While I was thinking about what Momma Williams asked me, I: Did Ever Think That I Would Have Three Babies, At One Time. The answer was an emphatically No, Hell No. I reminisces about the first day that I joined the Army, the special tactical team of transporting weapons and fuel, in the Army, then that day I was dam near killed, blown away then, there was UBER!

UBER came at me like a knight in White Armor, too safe a broken soul, a time too repent and get rid of all the old resentments and evil thoughts that I once had against the government, against people and against myself; all suddenly gone, taken out of my system, out of my way of conjuring up bad thoughts on how to get back at the Government for Cutting off one of my arms and my legs.

It was I, not UBER that caused my termination from a job that "Got Me Back On MY Feet"

Why, I did not have to go to The Army, it was my choice.

I did not have to take on a job with UBER, it was my choice.

I did not even have to go up to Sylvia's apartment that day and have that drink of wine, fall in love and get married and have children, I choose!

Now, the Wings of the Road are calling me back, UBER, UBER, UBER. Calling me back to take those that don't have much, like myself, and giving them a helping Hand. UBER is calling me back too drive for those that needed a small helping hand in getting to school, too work and to the airport, with not much money, but just the will to get out of their old ways and go smell the roses, do something new, something different; don't worry, The Wings of the UBER Mobile Will Get You There Safe and Sound…

"Mitch, just look at them, the boys look like Sylvia and the girl look like you"

Yeah, I can see that Sonya, but I wonder why the boys have all that hair and the baby girl has no hair"

"Oh, that's nature Mitch-she will have hair and the boys will lose their curly locks-Mitch, are you okay, do you need some coffee or something" said Salvo? as I was in a deep mode of meditation, looking at the babies through the glass of the neo-natal section of the hospital while Sylvia recovers.

"You have a fine family now son; two more and you'll have your own basketball team-say, how about those Lakers without Kobe" said Mr. Williams and I barely heard a word he said, still in a reminiscing mode.

"Mitch, have you and Sylvia decided on names for the babies," said Mrs. Williams.

"Oh, why, sort of-UBER and GROOVER, for the boys and sister sledge for the girl!

"What, you all 'ain't' naming my grandbabies after a car and that GROOVER name" said Mrs. Williams.

"The eighties & nineties, what ever time zone you are in son; you will never see times like that again" said Mrs. Williams.

"He lives in Hollywood Daddy, Mom; the babies may get a part in a movie with those names; how else will they be able to support three babies, not one, not two, but three babies, wow"! Said Sonya.

"Just kidding, and we will be able too take care of the babies just fine, even if I have too do a little moon-lighting driving for UBER again"

"UBER, you need to get UBER off your mind Mitchell, why I saw on the news while you all were in the delivery room that The Federal Government has filed a Law Suit against UBER and taking the company too Court"

"Really, I had not heard that what for"?

"Something too do with employment of their drivers Mitch; now don't get me wrong, but it seems like the drivers all got together and filed a Law Suit against UBER and now the Courts will here the case"

"Oh my, that is the case I was working on"

"You were working on, your not a lawyer Mitchell, how were you working on the case" said Salvo.

"The UBER drivers wrote letters to The Transportation Committee complaining about the conditions of being a partner instead of an employee without any benefits, for UBER"

"Well, your case just hit the news stations, that is all they are talking about-UBER is about to be Done, Son," said Mr. Williams.

I got to get back to Los Angeles to find out what is happening-UBER, must be saved, for the sake of the people!

Chapter XVIII

The Chase

"I think it will be a great idea Sylvia, that you stay here with your parents until the babies are able to fly in a Jet back too Los Angeles"

"Mitchell, what are you up too" Sylvia, being totally surprised, that now, I wanted her to stay in Atlanta, when I complained every night for three months or more her not being there in the bed with me.

"Oh, there are some legal things that I must do with UBER"

"UBER-you just can not get UBER off your mind-you are not working for UBER no more Mitch, so just concentrate on your new job"

"My new job, why anybody can do what I do at CLS, all they had too do is go to Radio Shack and get a application for a signal, like the one's that detect that a police is in the area with radar; rig it up to your cell phone and there, you got GOOGLE MAPS without paying a Billion Dollars a Year"

"If it were that simple they would have thought of it Mitch-you mean too tell me that they have gave you a position with a Limousine Driver, a private Lear Jet and a office with a secretary and all you do is give them a schematic of a Radio Shack Police Radar Sensor-oh come on Mitchell"

"Just about" The babies were crying for attention. They seemed to have heard our conversation about UBER. Already, they feel something is not right; UBER is growing in their memory just like it affected me-what the hell is a UBER, anyway? That is one thing that I must find out-where in the heck did that name come from and why can't I get it out of my memory?

"The babies are going to miss you Mitch-they love it when you talk to them, what is it that you say to them Mitchell that keeps them so quite, without giving them their bottle"?

"I tell them some of my UBER Stories"

"Mitchell, you have got to be kidding-all those stories that you use to tell me about your passengers that you picked up and made friends with, the babies just giggle and smile when you are talking to them"

"Yeah, maybe they know something that we do not know about UBER"

"What they know is that it is an Obsession of yours Mitchell and I don't want my babies growing up to be little UBER'ITTES, like their Daddy is a UBER'ATTE"!

"Okay honey, you know Sylvia, I see how much you like being home with your mom, dad and sister and I thought that it will be nice for us to consider moving here to Atlanta"

"Oh Mitchell, can we, I was going to bring that idea up too you, but I figured that you were so involved in your new job that it would put to much pressure on you"

"Oh, now honey, there are offices right here in Atlanta that I can work with getting the new system in-THE application into the Mobile Systems of the Limousine drivers right here in Atlanta"

"You would move Mitchell"

"Why yes, in a heart beat"

"Momma, Mitchell and I are moving here, too Atlanta" Sylvia yelled out to her mother who was in the Master bedroom down the hall.

"What was that Sylvia, you all are moving, when"

Oh boy, I must have opened a can of worms, now, when I get back to Los Angeles, I got to convince Chuck Jr that a much needed system of the Mobile Applications should be implemented right here in Atlanta. Just to think that Sylvia is always saying that I have an obsession with UBER, well she has an obsession with her mother and sister; those three are inseparable.

The mail was stacked up in my mailbox like cars on the 405 freeways, bumper to bumper; court papers for me to appear in the hearing against UBER. Well I thought that they forgot all about me and the plea to help the disabled veterans who have suffered immensely; already and now their pensions are being taken. Now I will have to gather all the previous cases against UBER and read them and know what I am talking about once I go to court. I have changed my stand against UBER from a driver that was previously against The SWEAT SHOP ON WHEELS too more having a cause and affect purpose to give information to people whom only wanted justice for the Veterans. The Chase Began… Back In Los Angeles with babies in toll….

"Mitch, we are going to have to hire a baby sitter, since I will be renting a booth to do hair and you will be at work" Adjusting, to a new wife, three new babies and a new job can be challenging, but when have been through HELL and back with UBER'S litigations, everything else is a piece of cake.

"Don't forget Sill (Sylvia), court today, downtown LA. we got to win this case in order for the Disabled Drivers can get their back pay"

"Does that include you Mitch, why, you use to work for UBER, and so if the Judge decides with the UNION, you will receive back pay also, right"

"Yes, that is right"

"We will use that money for the down payment on a house in Atlanta"

"You sure have a way of planning for our future honey; let's just keep our fingers crossed that the decision will be made in our favor"

"Mom and Dad called me and said they have picked us out the house that we will really like in Atlanta"

"Did they send pictures"?

"Yes, here they are"

"Wow, that is a big house-how much do they want for it"

"Four hundred and Eighty Five Thousand Dollar"

"A house that size will be going for over a million dollars out here in Los Angeles; tell your mom and dad that I like it and send them the down payment"

"Yeah, right, like you got that kind of money-you only been working for the new company for nine months Mitchell, now how are we going to get twenty percent down on a half a million dollar house"?

"One thing that I did not show you honey, it sort of slipped my mind but, the pension check for the injuries I suffered while in the Army, well, I never, ever touched a dime"

"What do you mean you never touched a dime-what have you been living off for the past twenty years"

"The Veterans Hospital-you sees, the housing is free, the meals are free and they gave us a clothing allowance-so, that money in in the bank on Wilshire and Twenty-Seventh Street; right down the street from the Veterans Hospital"

"What, well, that will mean, at Twenty-five hundred dollars a month, twelve months in a year-Mitch, you got over, Six Hundred Thousand Dollars in the Bank-just enough for the house"

"Just about-do you think we should pay cash or should we uses the Veterans Housing Bill"?

"Pay Cash, since, your work is not steady honey and these kids need a place to grow"

"Okay, I will find out who the realtor are in Atlanta and wire the money to the Escrow Company"

"Really, just like that"

"Something always told me to safe that money, out of fear that I would have to buy my own arm and legs and out of fear that the United States Government would abandon me; keep me crawling"

"They took good care of you Mitchell, now you can take good care of your family"

Southern Girl, why she knows how to Split Peas and stir up some buttermilk cornbread all at the same time-I am really blessed and what she gave too me could never be replaced by money.

"Hope you have a good day in court Mitch and I will call momma and tell her what your going to do about the house they picked for us"

"Love you, the babies and I will see you this evening, now, I got to cut to the Chase and get to The Federal Court House on Alameda and fourth street; one of my old pick up places while I was driving for UBER. Isn't that ironic, the place that I picked up passengers for UBER, now UBER is being summons for violation of the transportation LAWS...

Cutting to the chase, I drove myself, without all the Google Maps automatic custom guides and driving directions. I wanted to get a feel of the streets, the streets that I once chauffeured nearly One Thousand Passengers to their destinations. When those passengers were running late, I would cut to the chase and make any road possible, the road to get them their on time. Sometimes, even breaking the law by crossing over the double yellow lines and making U-Turns, in traffic, to drop off the client, on time, in front of their office or at the airport.

The roads were revengeful that morning, as I drove down Washington Boulevard, going east and looked at the street where I picked up a client that only needed a ride to Carl's Junior at six o'clock in the morning to buy some biscuits, yes biscuits, at Carls Junior Restaurant on Sepulveda and Pico. I thought that it was bizarre, a man, wearing short pants, standing on the corner, waiting for me to pick him up, to take him to Carl's Junior's to buy a biscuit. Until I dropped the man off, and I went through the drive through line and ordered those biscuits and sausage, and you know, that man was right; it was worth the Six Dollars and Eighty, Seven Cent ($6.87) that I earned to just taste and enjoy those Home made biscuits from Carl's Junior.

UBER had become a way of life; some people totally depended on UBER. Not the bus, not the Taxi services and not even walking two blocks to get to their destination, just UBER, I remembered, while I cut to the chase driving to the court house; the lady, young lady, that only wanted a ride two blocks to her mother's house and told me that it was too hot to walk, so she called the UBER system and logged in her trip, one way, to her mother's house. Two dollars and

Sixty Seven Cent, I earned for that ride. Yes, I was disgusted, since my end Of the week check totally depended on the miles driven, not the heat, not the person that I was picking up, just the miles that I drive.

Just to think, if the judge orders UBER to siege and exit their picking up and taking people to their destination for various reasons due to transportation violations, those people will lose a vital means of their transportation. If asked to testify, I will be totally truthful and take into consideration, the people that need UBER for their everyday life.

Chapter XIX

A Uberation, Liberation!

It was like a Hollywood Premier. The Federal Building, names after Ronald Wilson Reagan, now being plaque with UBER believers, UBERLIEVER'S, and the Dis believers of UBER (DISUBERLIEVERS).

"It's him, I can recognize that car any where, it's UBER-GROOVER" I could hear the protesters and the UBERLIEIVERS, why some recognized me a believer and some recognized me as a disbeliever of UBER. No matter what, I will tell the truth and how I felt about UBER and the techniques that UBER uses to "PIT" the pool of driver against each other on that STAR SYSTEM to get more mileage and competition from the driver. A brain washing technique that UBER used military and CIA agents no darn well that it is the old X Y Z theory of getting more production out of the driver by making them think that they will be rewarded for more riders, more miles, better politeness and professionalism toward the passengers although, the passengers were sometime belligerent and mean toward us drivers. It was a pitiful situation.

"Are you going to take the stand Grover?" said one of the students that I trained over nine months ago.

"James, how are you doing man"?

"Oh, still driving for UBER, waiting to see if we will get better benefits Mr. Martinez"

"How's your family"?

"I just added one more and now I have that Basketball Five-that's all; I heard that you had kids Mr. Martinez"

"Why yes" I said, as I was surprised that the driver I trained knew so much about my personal life.

"Fight for us Mr. Martinez, tell them how we were cheated out of our hard driving hours and the wear and tear that we have just making ends meet, without any benefits"

"I will tell the judge all that I know…." Just then, I was cut short with the protesters singing an erythematic song about UBER…

UBER, UBER, WE DRIVE LONG, CAN YOU HEAR US, ALL NIGHT LONG UBER, UBER, UBER, WE GOT NOTHING, JUST GIVE US A LITTLE SOMETHING, NO, MEDICAL, NO DENTAL, WE GOT NO WORK MAN'S COMP, BUT WE CAN NOT STOP, DRIVING FOR UBER IS EVIL, WHILE $50,000,000.00 DOLLARS MADE BY STEVEL.

UBER, UBER, JUST GIVE US A LITTLE SOMETHING, DON'T LEAVE US DRIVERS WITH NOTHING…

Pretty witty, I acclaimed, the UBER drivers and the Taxi drivers and all the other transportation drivers, of course were behind the UBER DRIVER'S KNOWING THAT IF THE UBER DRIVER'S RECEIVE MORE PAY WITH BENEFITS, THERE GOES UBER AS A VIABLE SOURCE IN THE COMMUNITY.

THE OPENING STATEMENTS AGAINST AND FOR UBER:

The run was rapid, inside the courtroom, as the federal attorney against The UBER Transportation group read all the complaints to the Presiding Judge. The speed was rapid, just like when, as a driver, you get that call and you accept the mission and you are pointed to the destination pick up point.

The chase began, as I looked and there were several attorneys representing UBER, like a POOL of Passengers, that, I once carried to and from the cities.

"Your honor, there are over two hundred citations that UBER has violated" said the Federal Attorney, Laurel Mitten.

"Your honor, all of the allocations and the insinuations are all false, since they have never been charged" said the defense team for UBER, a Samuel Smith, whom wore a long beard and a faded suit from the early sixties; like the one that I still hang in my storage closet. Running through all kinds of different programs that UBER has started, The Flu Shot program where a UBER driver gives the community members rides to the pharmacy and or the nurse escorts the driver to give the passengers a flue shot.

UBER has done a great deal for the community, but it appeared those community health care programs and AIDS awareness was promoted too keep the Feds from their REAL Issues and that was: BREAKING FEDERAL TRANSPORTATION LAWS.

Listening to all the various charges and listening to the defense team reminded me of those first few weeks when I started driving for UBER. The attorneys cut to the chase like I did, gun whole, to take on the mission; not slowing down until their client is satisfied, just like I did for the UBER company; professional, integrity and making my point and their point on completing the mission.

UBER is getting a piece of their own medicine, since all that improper information and deeds were exposed. UBER, setting up Transportation Company hiring any and everybody that had a valid license, with a four-door vehicle and that vehicle passing an inspection. The background check was fragile and only went back five years. Molesters, Murderers and Convicted Felons could drive for UBER any day out of the week, as Laurel Smith, the attorney that took two hours going over all the allocations against UBER.

Four hours of continued accusations and litigations against UBER, Never has a company been placed on the spotlight; there has never in the history of transportation and commerce, a company that, everyday, in the news, each and everyday, law suits, each and everyday a accident involving a UBER driver, either running over a pedestrian or crashing their vehicle into a fire hydrate or another car.

UBER, was in for an Over-Haul; A UBER-HAUL.

The attorney's rested their case and no witnesses for or against UBER was called to testify-it was all in the proceedings and the evidence spoke for itself, against and/ or for UBER…

The Judge retired into his Chambers and all throughout the city, people were waiting to hear the Judge's decision, just like people anticipated the O J Simpson decision. Everyone was in suspense.

Chapter XX

A Uberration!

THE FEDERAL GOVERNMENT TRIUMPTED, OVER UBER, IN THE JUDGE DECISION…

1. BACKPAY FOR ALL UBER DRIVERS THAT DROVE FOR UBER.
2. WORKMAN'S COMPENSATION, FOR UBER DRIVER'S THAT WERE
3. MEDICAL AND DENTAL INSURANCE, ALL PAID BY UBER…
4. FUEL COMPENSATION FOR ALL DRIVERS.
5. MAINTENANCE STIPEND FOR UBER DRIVER'S.

The list went on and on and UBER stood to lose $300,000,000 (Three Hundred Million Dollars) in compensation to all 75,000 UBER drivers.

Federal fines accumulated to $250,000,000; Two Hundred and Fifty Million.

Suspension of all UBER driven vehicles until license, inspections and vehicles are available by the UBER Company, to the driver's; UBER cannot use the driver's personal vehicle.

UBER, must furnish the drivers with Smart Phones once a vehicle is furnished to the drivers…

UBER has until 2018, to have all the court ordered changes completed, or The UBER Company will be dismantled permanently.

Outside the Ronald Reagan Federal Court House, cheers rung out, over coming the Boo's, that some regretted UBER was dealt with so harshly, while other's, such as The Taxi Service, The Limousine Services, The Municipal Bus Services, were cheering until they were as Red as a Traffic Light.

"We did it Mr. Martinez, we made the difference in the decision of our benefits" said Brian and with Shymara, two of the disabled veterans that I trained while I worked for UBER; Shymara, holding on too Brian's shoulder, Since she is Blind, to my utter surprise, was there at the Court House, not seeing, but taking in all the information with GOOGLE Cell Phone.

"The decision was made-fair for some and unfair for others; that is the way of the world," I told the group of former UBER Drivers, as I ignored the rest of the crowd, some celebrating, that they just took down a GIANT, of THE PEOPLE'S TRANSPORTATION, all for their own selfish needs and wants.

"Grover, what will we do now; we can not afford the cab services, we can not catch the buses anymore once we were used to having door to door services from UBER; we were spoiled, we want our UBER BACK!" Said some of the passengers who were standing outside the courthouse. How did they recognize me and called me out as the Grover, of the once called UBER-I have no idea.

"We are having a get together at THE GRAND, downtown Grover; will you come and say a few words to our UNION" said a Taxi Company Driver, that I recognized from my time when I drove for UBER, while we waited at The cell Parking those days to get our assignments. The Taxi service by dispatch, and UBER got its calls through the cell phone services.

"Sure, I will go and see what is going on now with the Unions and what is in stored for all the Transportation Driver's" I told Mohammed; why thinking back, he was the Taxi Driver that EGG'ED my Malibu. I was surprised they did not export him out of the country. Well, the union is stronger than steel in this part of the country.

"Thank you, Grover, for writing those letters to The Transportation Department and making them aware of the problem" another transportation driver told me as I was passing through the crowd.

The Times Magazine wrote up a full article of THE UBER, GROVER'S letters to the department of transportation and all the complaints that I informed the newspaper editorial section and they published those interviews and documents right in The Sunday paper-that is the reason people are calling me their hero, their political savior and their spokesperson.

UBER, is a total mess-why didn't they go the legal way, the right way and the safe and sound way in putting a great idea for the misrepresented people to ride, instead of using those GHETTO TACTICS in selling their UBER PASSES on CRAIG"S list and just letting any person just get in the back of your vehicle, talk trash to the driver, ASSAULT the driver and go on there separate ways.

My cell phone rung constantly. I received a call from Larry, then Carl, more than likely they wanted to discuss the decision by the federal court. I looked on my caller I.D. and there was my wife, I took the call immediately…

"Mitchell, I saw you coming out of the court house, congratulations on the decision by the courts"

"Oh, it wasn't only me, there were a lot of people involved in getting fair benefits to the drivers and safety for the driver of UBER" I told Sylvia.

"Are you on your way home" she said. I know what that means, another reward. The babies are three months old now and Sylvia has a strong appetite for SEX. I will skip the UNION meeting and go back home and spend time with my family. They are my Union and I got to represent them now…

"Be there shortly honey, just taking the Surface Streets Home-you know how I like just seeing the old passengers that I use to drive going about their everyday business, in going to the airport, going to school and to work"

"Well Mitch, what I saw on the news is UBER was hit hard on it's violations; why there were over one hundred transportation violations that UBER, must fix before the government will let UBER take to the road again"

"I know honey, but, all that I can do now, is continue TO GROOVE, with my music and taking that drive through the streets of Los Angeles"

"Your grooving days are done Mitch, now you come on home and help me with these babies-I sure will be happy when Escrow closes on the home in Atlanta-bring some pampers home Mitch, these babies go through diapers like a V-8 car drinking gas, all up, in seconds, need to make a change, make a pit stop-by the way Mitch, will you get paid for the maintenance and the gas that you put into your vehicle while you drove for UBER"

"Oh yes, that's right-I can be expecting a check straight into my account, any day now"

"I got it all figured out Mitch-you drove for UBER for a year and used approxamently fifty dollars a day and you drove seven days a week so they owe us, oh, I mean you baby-that rounds out too over Two Thousand Dollars"?

"Just about baby, just about-be there soon honey, I will pick up three loads of pampers on my way-do you need milk"

"I have plenty of milk, Mitch, just waiting for you, not the babies-you know that the babies use Similac, get a few cans of Similac Mitch and hurry up, the babies need changing"

"Okay, be there a.s.a.p. Bye"

Oh well, as I thought to myself; one situation leads to another. Looking back, I always treated my young passengers with the most respect, not knowing that I would be nurturing my own three children one day. Maybe God was preparing me for this; three babies, wow. I remember when I use to pick up the college students and take them too their classes; I offered them water and I always had some corn chips and potato chips in the car, just for them. I sensed that the college students were having a difficult time studying for their finals at California State University, Long Beach, so I use to cheer them up and tell them: Study Hard, for your test, you do not want to be a driver, you want someone to drive you in your life young man, young lady.

What would have happened if I had not got my legs and arm blown the hell off-why, those same CEO's and Managerial and Directors of the Top Fortune 500 Businesses that I picked up and drove to the airport and too their staff meeting, why I would have been one of them; in the back seat of a Limousine or a UBER car. I use to listen to their conversations and how they used that well-defined language of businessman; the profit margins, the cost benefits analysis and the productivity. Well, when they were dropped off at those fine hotels, I use to remember those words they used and wrote those words down and GOOGLE'D them on my Smart phone. Why, I did not get my MBA from Harvard or Berkeley, but I got my knowledge from The Streets of Hard Bumps In The Road, Driving for UBER…

Oh well, look at their faces now-life in the future, without UBER; I know darn well that those CEO's for UBER will not even turn a corner with what they are Demanded to repair in the Federal Court Decision; why those young BUCKS are sitting on Fifty-Billion Dollars $50,000,000,000, and all they will do is hire a team of attorneys to appeal and appeal and appeal again and again.

The federal Marshalls will impound each and every UBER vehicle on the road and confiscate their High Technological Data Base, when those UBER executives do not give into the Federal Mandate. How do I know these things? Well, with twenty years of reading the stock market, the Los Angeles Times and watching CNN and Fox news, why I have seen those Big Ballers Come and Go, and UBER is no different. They took the High Road and winded up in a cul-de-sac and now they got to go back to that stop light after making a U-Turn, and re-think their business plans.

The same old game with a different name. The Madddol, Billion Dollar Posey Scam that took over Five Hundred Billion Dollars from Investors, was one the biggest scams of the Century. The ZZZ company scam that tricked the people that invested millions of dollars into a business that was fictitious and then, the Granddaddy of them all was the Housing and Bank Predatory Scam that collapsed the housing market and the banking system and almost cost the entire country to collapse. Well, I seen and lived through them all and The UBER Scam may out source them all, since UBER is all over the entire world now and once people dial up a car too pick them up and get no answer: What Will They Do.

The Taxi Cab Company is all out of business from UBER. The fleet of Buses are in the retirement yard, since the bus drivers were all laid off, due too the people that just stop taking the bus and found it more convenient to take the UBER car; and then those Rickshaws in India, China, The Philippines and all those Third World Countries are all Trashed and put in The Dumps, why they are all destroyed because of UBER. People will have too walk to work and to school now if they want to be on time; that's how life goes and that is how things work on the Roads too UBERGATE! End of the Road....

Chapter XXI

Part II

THE UBER-MOVER INTERVIEW
WITH
ROLLING STONE MAGAZINE
(YEAR 2017)

At the plush Eylse on Melrose and Doheny, Rolling Stone Writer Edward Synder, set up a interview with me, the most popular Uber-Mover of all times. With a total of Eight Hundred Five Stars and rating of 4.89, no other Uber-Mover could touch the class, the integrity and the professionalism that I rendered to each and every passenger that I drove for the past two years. A official count of Fifteen Hundred passengers within a year and a half while driving two-Google, special equipped self driving vehicles, I set the record World Wide on how driving for the clients, whether they are being transported three blocks or three hundred miles to Las Vegas, Nevada, all riders were treated the same in my vehicle.

"So, your saying that even if it was a $3.00 three dollar or a $300.00 dollar ride on what you explained to me, a Surge to Las Vegas, Nevada, you treated all of your clients the same way Mr. Martinez" said Edward S.

"That's correct, I made sure that they had enough leg room and there was cold water in the back seat with some mints, not chocolate, but specific, mints, since chocolate got all over the upholstery from the riders sloppy eating habits, "You say, cold water, how did you keep the water cold, I am just wondering" "There is a cooler in the back seat of the arm rest of my UBER-GOOGLE vehicle that I controlled from the front instrument panel-sometimes, during a heat wave, I would place chilled sprite, Gatorade and Perrier water in the back cooler for the riders"

"Wow, I would have liked to have been your rider when I rode a UBER-CAR; now, tell me Mr. Martinez, did you pay for the little luxuries of having everything but caviar for the customers" the interviewer said, being sarcastic.

"Yes, it was all on me, but I was paid back very handsomely"

"How is that"?

"Tips"

"Well, I thought that the UBER-Drivers policy was not too accept tips"

"Yes, that was the policy and the company, if the tips were paid for on the UBER Application once the passenger logged out, UBER, would not give that tip to the driver-that was just one of the two hundred law suits that UBER lost in the past five years when The Drivers took UBER to Court in a Class Action Law Suit"

"Let's talk about that Law Suit Mr. Martinez"

"Just call me Mitch"

"Well Mitch-tell me more about the Law Suit that you spear headed that took the UBER Company Millions upon Millions to settle the Class Action Law Suit"

"I speared headed; it was UBER that exploited the drivers, like me, so Karma caught up with UBER"

"Karma-by the way, what does UBER really stand for-do you mind if I have a bottle of Perrier from the wet bar"

"Help yourself, your company is paying for all of this, even the meals during the interview"

"Oh really"

"Sure, you think that I could ever afford a seven hundred dollar a night room making three dollars and fifty seven cent an hour on the average from my previous UBER salary"

"Oh, come on Mitch-no one is crazy enough to have excepted a hourly wage below ten dollars"

"Well I did, look, these are my old salary print outs, see for your self"

"Well I be damn, it is no wonder that UBER settled the case, you drivers received less, by far than the minimum wage, but didn't you know that"

"We knew it, but UBER, by then, became a Cult; A MOBILE CULT"

"Wait a minute, first you tell me that your drivers were exploited, which I can see here from the papers, then you tell me that you were Hypnotized to drive for UBER-how is that Mitch, say, do you mind if I order lunch"

Well, why not-"Rolling Stone magazine will gather no Moist," if you do not indulge yourselves.

A minute by minute interview with The popular but controversial Rolling Stone Magazine exposed UBER at it's Finest hour, as I accounted for, by all my personal records and news paper articles that I kept to cover my own ass revealed how UBER Transcended me and others to a state of mind to drive for UBER, Be committed to UBER and Dam near Die for UBER!

After several listening to my conscious relief that Synder wrote down and looked at the transcripts from the more than two hundred law suits that UBER accumulated over the last seven years I became mesmorized & memorized as I can remember the first time I drove for UBER.

"Boy that was a good meal-steak well done and lobster"

"Yes in deed, it was a two hundred dollar meal on the bill of The Rolling Stones account-by the way, will you just initial the bill Mr. Snyder"

"Why sure, after all, they will not take the money out of my account like UBER did you drivers-I can not believe that they deducted, each and every week, the money charged for the Background check, they deducted the taxes charged by the city airports and they deducted their own UBER Insurance payments from The UBER DRIVER account-but you, you still drove and you drove for more than One Thousand passengers" said Snyder.

"Passengers, is that what you said, I had over One thousand passengers in the two years that I drove for UBER, that I did"

"So, what your telling me and I am judging from the expression on your face, you continued to drive, not for the little or no money, you drove for the people, the passengers"

"You Got That Right-I can remember what a rewarding and wonderful conversations I had with the passengers-you can not imagine how much the people that sat in my back seat had in common with me-there was only thirty six inches of separation between me and the passengers in the back seat and three degree's of separation-3-D" I reminisced and began to tell Synder about my own experience with UBER.

Flashback:

It was in the spring of Twenty-Fourteen, when they rehabilitation counselor approached me after I was finally equipped with the new Johnson and Johnson Prostatic Plastic Arm and two legs.

"Arm and two legs-you mean to tell me that you are a paraplegic" Synder interrupted me while I was thinking back to the time I was depressed and use to watch all the employee's come in to their jobs with their arms and legs telling their stories how they enjoyed their weekends with their families and friends while I was stuck at The Veterans Medical Center, West Los Angeles being sized up for new legs and a arm.

"Why yes, didn't you read the summary before you accepted the assignment"

"I must have skipped it-wow, Mitch, do you mind if I take a look at the Prosthetics, I mean, the legs that they made for you" as I looked at Synder, and I thought, well, if it will help other veterans and other people that want to pursue a career in transportation by reading the magazine article that The Rolling Stone publishers will put out world wide-I dropped my pants all the way down and Synder was Startled.

Synder stared at the bolts, the curves and the screws and I gathered that he never seen such a work of art; to Synder, if he was looking observing a Picasso Painting or The Mona-Lisa for the first time, thinking, how was it done, how did such mechanics, such craftsmanship and technology came together.

"Mitch, do you mind, I hate to ask you this, but do you mind if I take a picture for the article"

He asked me with dignity and respect, so I allowed Synder to take pictures of me standing with the Plastic

Legs, front and back and sitting and a full view up to my skivvies (Underwear) where the plastic fitted into my suffered legs that had healed over the years but was a stub. Synder webbed openly.

I didn't have to take my shirt off for him to see my left missing arm, but I would have. I was afraid that he may have gotten depressed enough to stop the interview.

"They need to see this, what those bastards did to you-the UBER Company, did they not have any compassion in letting you drive for them and you only made pennies after sacrificing your life and your legs to fight for freedom"

"UBER did not do this, it was Politics that took my Legs, my dignity and my Life from me Synder," I told him.

"But, those dishearten corporate devils, how did they expect you to drive over one thousand passengers in pain, in agony and not even getting the minimum wages-did they feel that you were just a commodity, a slave to making them their quota, and their stock pile of Sixty-Eight Billion Dollars in Profit"

"I volunteered"

"You what" said Snider, as he was getting more and more distraught.

"I agreed to take on the risk, the consequences and the pain I received-it was me, not UBER or the Federal Government-I volunteered, just like I volunteered to join the military after those terrorist attacks, it was me and now, I am not in denial, the pleasure of driving was mine when, especially when I first started driving and looked at the cell phone to who I was to pick up as a rider and females, the female riders really got my dander up"

"What was that Mitch-oh, excuse me for breaking down like that, it was very unprofessional of me-now you say, the females, your passenger females, that is what kept you moving"?

"You see Snider, once I lost my legs and arm, my senses increased 100 percent, my sensory cells; it was a protective mechanism"

"You mean to tell me that when a woman, the women riders, you could read them by just smelling them as they got into your vehicle"

"Yes, that is right-I could tell what shampoo they used in their hair, it could smell if they had sex that night or that morning; I smelled them and their body odor, all good, to me and I loved it when they got into the back of my car and I drove them to their destination-it was a man's thing that was lost, the sense of smell and I was very acutely aware of that and I use to test if I was right about their shampoo's and the perfume they used by, on my spare time from driving, I use to go into The Mall and spray some perfume on the cards and sniff it and then I would go into Target and Macy's and smell the different products. I was right 100 percent of the time and I could even tell, when I got good at it when the women were on their menstrual and before they have their menstrual periods"

"How could you tell if they were about to have their menstrual Mitch"?

"The shadow under their eyes"

"Oh, so you used your extra sensory of sight"

"It was nothing extra about it-you see Synder, when a women is about to have their Menstrual cycle the blood pulls down from the brain to each and every blood vale and it leaves shadows, some dark and some light under the females eyes-yes, I could tell; I looked at them through the rear view mirror when

I drove and when I greeted them and announced: UBER, I am your UBER Driver"

"Wow, for two years of your driving for UBER, you really used all of what you had, all of what you gained from all your tragedies and it was to your advantage Mitch"

"Yes, I had plenty of sexual propositions"

"Sex"

"Yes, Sex"

"As a driver, you mean to tell me that you solicited women"

"No, never-they use to leave me their numbers and asked me questions of what my nationality was"

"Your nationality-what do you mean? -Wait a minute, out of tape, let me change the tape"

"Say Synder, let's go to the pool side and get some fresh air-it is a beautiful day and we can have a few drinks at the pool site"

"Sounds like a good thing to me-now, I have my recorder and my pen and paper-let's go Mitch"

We left the room as I place the card on the door for the room service to come in and take the food tray and clean up the room while Synder and I went downstairs to the pool.

"What's wrong?" I asked Synder, as we walked to the long halls of the most elegant Hotel in Beverly Hills.

"I could not help but watch you walking; I am sorry but when I took a look at your prosthetic legs, I could not help but too observe your walking abilities"

"I get a lot of that-people look, kids come up to me and want to see with there little eyes at my plastic legs when I do not have any long pants on-it does not bother me in the least-I am use to it now"

"Did you see that"?

"See what Synder"

"That lady, why she stared you down as if she wanted too say something too you"

"The one that just got off the elevator"

"Why, yes"

"I get a lot of that too, they act as if I am a Movie Star, a Celebrity, especially when I was in this area of Beverly Hills driving for UBER"

"Now I get it-that is why those ladies use to leave you their number; they wanted to know you"

"There is a severe shortage of men that are straight in this area of Hollywood and Beverly Hills, so why wouldn't they give me a stare down Synder"

"Oh, that's what it is-but I see something different-the girls are all in that industry; the movies, the music and they do not have time to establish a relationship these days, they just want a man for that moment"

"Yeah, but I am happily married"

"That's right, and I do remember that you stated in your letter you meant your wife while driving for UBER"

"That's right-the best thing that ever came out of Driving UBER, and now I am a UBER-MOVER"

"Why do you say that"?

"I use to be a UBER-GROOVER and now I am a UBER-MOVER, they difference is I have gotten to old and I have a different perspective on life now that I am married with three children"

"Three children, why, when you contacted us and we researched the UBER Law suits, you just got married and now you have three children"

"Yes, I hit the lottery when I had three babies all at the same time"

"Triplets"

"That's right"

"Why you lucky fellow"

"Lucky-well I would just say that I put all my eggs in one basket and they all cracked the Code of Life; they swam like little ducklings and finally penetrated the mother load egg"

"You are really hilarious-now tell me, when you were not married, since we are on the subject, did you ever date are have a relationship with any of those female riders"?

"No, that never happened, only because either they are I wanted a commitment, but, I had a lot of offers"

"I bet you did-I can see how women are really attracted to you"

"Like wise I am sure"

"I am gay Mitch"

"Well, I had male and female propositions but I am straight"

"Oh, just my luck" said Synder and we continued the interview.

Chapter XXII

The Uber-Movers

At a temperature of eighty-seven degree's, Mitch worked the crowd, as I observed him as if he was a Rock Star. What a article this will turn out to be; what a opportunity for a Brit like me; graduate of Oxford school of Journalism and now, doing my first real interview with the man they once called: The UBER-GROOVER, since he initiated the highest paid Law Suit that the World has ever seen against the UBER Partnership Corporation. A mere cell phone application system with the help of Goggle Apps that made Billions upon Billions of dollars by just having willing and able driver, from their own neighborhoods pick up and drop off riders.

"They are treating you like a rock star Mitch"

"Most of the people right here at this Hotel, I have driven them to their homes in Compton, Long Beach and Hollywood; you see Synder, with the high price of parking in the Hollywood and Beverly Hills area workers, just took the UBER to work and home each and everyday. A few of the workers even sold their cars with the high price of insurance, taxes on their vehicle and believe it or not, gas was almost five dollars a gallon"

"Wow, that's why they love you here and everywhere else"

"That is why they love UBER"

"So what went wrong-I mean, why did the drivers as yourself, decided to sue UBER and won a multi-billion dollar case"

"Movers, that is all they were concern about; those administrators that ran the apps and kept pressing the drivers to do more and more, pick up more and more people, drive, drive, drive without any benefits, UBER did not pay for the gas; UBER did not pay for the maintenance and UBER did not care for the drivers that made them in the Billions of Dollars"

"You mean to tell me that a Billion Dollar a year company did not share there wealth although it was the most popular transportation system in the entire world Mitch"

"That is why we sued, and UBER, when they lost the Law suit that they claimed that they were partners with the drivers but as a partner, the wealth must be shared and that was the reason the drivers, such as myself won the case"

"Over a few martinis, Mitch and I discussed all the formication's of how the UBER Company was set up, knowing, that the drivers, not the riders, not the administrators of the company and not the owner and CEO's, were setting up the drivers and the drivers only like Hitler brained washed his Nazi Troops to think that they were superior and tried too take over the world-UBER brain washed and exploited people, the drivers, like the Furor exploited the entire world; LYING."

The lying of the UBER administrators, the low pay, on the average four dollars per ride and the lack of benefits, but Mitch Drove On and was a Major Mover of the Transportation Giant UBER. Why did Mr. Mitch Mitchell stay on with the UBER team of drivers after being suspended and then rehired, since the federal law prohibits anyone that was in the Class Action Law Suit, could not be terminated; Mitch Mitchell Drove On!

"Well Mitchell, I am going to call it a evening, besides, I am out of tape, so I am going to retire in my room and will see you tomorrow morning"

"That's fine Synder; I will be up later; I just like to stay here and watch the people; the people from the Movie Industry staying right here in the Elyse' Hotel and the people that are in the Music Industry all gather here and make there moves to make millions"

"Yeah, that they do, that they do-but if you keep telling the story, and if everything checks out correct, The Movers will not be able to Groove no more throughout the world"

"It will never happen"

"What"

"Uber, is like OBAMA, The PEOPLE"S CHOICE"

"I will have to remember that-but for now, I am getting some rest; that Jet Lag has taken its toll on me"

"Okay-see you at breakfast time"

"Sure"

As I left Mitch at the pool side of the Elyse' Hotel, I was wondering if he could swim with those Plastic Legs-probably not-it looks like they weigh a ton and he would sink straight to the bottom of the pool-Mitch will have to take the prosthetics off and then take a dive in the pool-I wonder how the people would accept that who are swimming? Here is a man that gave his life to fight for freedom and the people will never accept those scares he got by losing his legs.

One o'clock in the morning, I heard music and laughter; it was Mitchells room. The noise would not stop so I knocked and knocked on the adjoining room, only separated by a locked, sliding door at the prestige's Hotel Elyse in Beverly Hills.

"Mitch-what is going on in there, are you okay"

"Yeah, come on and join us, we are getting giggly with our UBER stories"

"What-why is one thirty in the morning and you have company"

"That's right- we were waiting for you to wake up and smell the fresh roses Synder-come on in to the party"

There were three women, wearing Laggins but well designed dresses inside Mitchell's room.

"Synder, this is the lovely Samantha and Cynthia and Marie; a few of my former UBER clients"

"You don't say-why, it is good to meet you and you, Mitch, you have decided to have a party or a 'UBERThon'"

"More like a UBER-Thong, just look at these beautiful women Snider-now you can not tell me that driving UBER is the greatest connection in the entire world"

"How many of those martini's have you had Mitch"?

"Oh, he has had at least ten while we were swimming nude in the pool" said one of the girls that I assumed her name was Cynthia, with a tattoo that spelled CYN of a female all nude on her left arm.

"You, why you swam Mitch, in the pool"

"Why sure, just because I have no legs and one arm does not mean I am Dead, Yet-I can swim like a fish Old Boy, now come on, get that mic and get over here and start interviewing these babes on UBERING"

"Why, sure, that will be a splendid idea, give me a minute while I go back to my room and get my recorder-now, you gals have driven in a UBER vehicle before"

"I have done everything in a UBER; Sex, Smoked Dope and even Masturbated in the back seat of a UBER" said Marie, the beautiful blond that could very well be a model, if it were not for her scar on her left knee that looked rather annoying as I wanted to ask her where did she get such a distasteful scar that was very noticeable as I looked up at her beautiful face, her couture coke shape body and then, as she was wearing a very revealing skirt, that scar, that ugly scar on her right knee that took away all her beauty in a snap shot of a flash bulb.

"Oh really, so I take it that you three ladies are of the night, I mean, working gals" I asked very auspiciously and not to get into their personal business, but what kind of women would be dressed as if they were on The Cat Run at a Show in the middle of the morning at this five start hotel-I was not naive and did not pretend to be anything else but stupid.

"They are my regulars Synder, you see, once I got to know them, I would get a personal call from them on my cell phone for a pick up-then, I would take them, sometimes all three of them and sometimes just one or two of my UBER BABES to their destination whether it was Charlie Sheen or Gwen Pathrow house, they knew how to please a client, just like I did in my professional driving"

"Well, you don't say" I told the UBER-Unusual guest, not knowing that I have struck a Gold Mine in my article that, since this morning, there were only two more days remaining before I would have to fly back to London and edit and submit this uncanny story to The Publishers at Rolling Stone.

"Now tell me ladies; has Mitchell, well, if it is okay with you too ask your UBER Mistresses, have Mitchell ever indulged with you three ladies in any way"

"Mitch, oh no, he is a brown teddy bear and I just love too put my fingers in his curly hair but that is why we always called on Mitch for a ride; he has never, ever tried to make a pass at me or my friends; he always kept his driving profession out of his pleasures" said Cynthia, as the other girls, now, after a few questions, went straight to the wet bar and took a few drinks out and started pouring them into a fine crystal glass compliments of Rolling Stone.

"I truly commend you Mitchell-so, besides from your UBER rides, did the UBER Driver, Mitchell act as a, sort of protector, like a PIMP, sort of speak"

"Escort, for us, we have no Pimps, we work only for our selves"

"Okay ladies" I could see after they indulged in a few drinks on the house they started taking off their shoes and their dresses and pulled out the convertible bed plopped on the mattress and Cynthia and Maria just dozed off to sleep-I guess Mitch invited them up for the uncanny interview and told them they could stay and for them to make themselves comfortable.

If this is what UBERING is all about, I would have to say the life style is fantastic and if I were not persuasive of the other gender, I would have certainly joined in the mascaraed of joyful pleasantries.

All asleep, as I looked at them before retiring to my room and I thought to myself, they are in the same Pool of People; the prostitutes and the paraplegics, duped by society, all four, Mitchell, Cynthia, Maria and the other young lady, had a promising young life and then, something or somebody "Crashed" their party by subjecting them to a unforeseen situation. A war, a proposition to do better for themselves by taking a chance and going against the grain. Now look at them, one with no legs and one arm, and the three on the streets with scares that they carry for the rest of their life, from their past mistakes.

UBER, united them; by creating a system that transport them from one whore house to the next for little are nothing and a driver, Mitchell, who suffered a dramatic war time experience and the only opportunity ever given back to him was too drive the whores, drive the drug dealers and the Drive By Shooters in South Central Los Angeles to their destinations without questioning The UBER Administrators. What an anomalies, what a unforseable situation, that is getting ready to explode.

UBER, will not work with the system that was created on a flute due to the exploitation of the drivers and the awards of the passengers that were pitted against each other to move the driver to a better situation by getting monetary funds while moving the passengers to their destination for little or nothing in payments while they thought that they can take fully advantage of the cheap fare. When the fares increase once the Law Suit is paid out and the riders are subject to pay a greater amount than the bus and yellow cab system, UBER will be in more trouble.

Chapter XXIII

The Ultimate Mover/UBER

"Saddle up" I could hear the knocking on my door and Mitch telling me to "Saddle Up"

"What in tarnation are you talking about now Mitchell"? I was still sleeping after an uneventful night with the Confessions of a UBER Rider; those three young and beautiful damsels gave me the story of a lifetime. After recording them I spent the remaining part of the morning placing the information on my Laptop and emailing at least half of the dialogue that I collected to The Headquarters at Rolling Stone Publications, in London, England.

"Time to get started on the road so that you can see, you can smell and you can be part of The UBER MOVERS' Mr. Sydney Edward Synder" said Mitchell, already dressed with his legs on and trousers too boot.

"The girls, what happened too them-did they leave already"

"Yeah, they had breakfast on your tap and they caught them a UBER back to their house in Brentwood"

"Brentwood, isn't that an exclusive area of Los Angeles-how does some hookers afford to live in Brentwood Mitchell"? Now, slipping out of the sack and fighting my way to the bathroom and brushing my teeth before showering as Mitchell talked to me through the door of the lavish Renaissance Style Bathroom with two separate bowls and a button to spray the ass once I have contributed to the waste of Beverly Hills.

161

"Easy, my English friend; they use UBER for their transportation and save thousands a night"

"They make that kind of money"

"Sometimes, they have a roll of one hundred dollar bills and they have me take them to the night deposit at their banks"

"Well, UBER has created a system of welfare for the riders and for the driver; I just know that you get a handsome tip once you have waited on them all night outside their clients house"

"You got that right Synder-now let's go, we are doing the UBER thing today"

"Really" I said in total surprise, since I thought that Mitchell was suspended from UBER driving but it turned out that he was still in the system after the Federal Courts ruled that those that have testified during the court case could not be suspended and or fired from their job working as a driver for UBER.

"Your ready"

"Ready as I am going to be-where are we headed"?

"Anywhere that there is a POOL PICK-UP"

"A POOL-PICK-UP, what do you mean"

"A POOL PICK-UP is where the rider choses to stop and pick up other passengers on their way to their destinations for a lower fare" said Mitch.

"How much lower can a fare be-why they are getting rides at the expense of the drivers for pennies when the drivers pay for the gas, the maintenance and for the insurances" I was startled when Mitch told me that there was even a lower fare.

"You will be the Pool rider once we pick up other riders Snyder-just be casual and watch what you say"

"Wow, I think that is a great idea Mitch, hands on experience as a rider for UBER-now I can get to the MEAT of the MATTER"

"What do you mean Synder"?

"Well, after researching some of the accusations about UBER and the newspaper and television captions of UBER drivers being KILLED, UBER drivers being beat up and UBER drivers suing the company; I got to ask myself the most salient question: WHY DRIVE"

It's in the Ride, the chase to pick up the rider, it is in the different experiences of meeting the people that you drive from all walks of life-UBER is a Life Change"

"Let Me"

"What"

"LET ME-Drive for UBER, I want to quit my job working for The Rolling Stones Magazine and apply to be a UBER Driver-you see Mitch, I always wanted to be a War Correspondent and I use to love the trills and the chills of THE ULTIMATE CHASE-I would like being a UBER DRIVER, I want too quit my job as a Journalist and Drive for UBER"

"Wait a minute Snyder, just because you see me with the most beautiful women in Los Angeles and just because you see me lodging at the most expensive Hotels in Los Angeles and just because I can work when ever I want too and take off and go back to Atlanta where my wife and children live, when ever I please, does not mean this kind of life style is for you are anybody else"

"I fit the mode, the criterion and I want you too show me today the technology that UBER uses and I want too pay attention to your charm and your eloquence and how you always receive those FIVE STARS OF EXCELLENT DRIVING from your riders"

"That can't be learned, it's 'innate', not acquired Snyder"

"Your mad, your jealous, why can't you show me-I can be a driver just like you, why are there over Seven-Hundred and Fifty-Thousand Driver throughout the entire world and Seventy five thousand in the United States alone-why can't I drive for UBER" I asked Mitch.

"Synder, the turn over of drivers is tremendous, they are always asking for more and more drivers since they do not last long at the wheel"

"Well, I want to be a Mover, a UBER Mover, like you; you are The Best GROOVER of the Movers"

"Your funny, but too be the best, and you have indicated that you wanted to be a War Correspondent-so, to be like me, you got to be a Amputee"

"What the hell, are you kidding me-do you think that I am joshing you Mitch-why what a thing to say-you have suffered so much and now you say I got to go to the war and get my legs and my arm blown off to be a Excellent Driver"?

"Look Synder-here comes the car from valet by the way, get the tip ready-look, all I am trying to tell you is-most of my passengers feel sorry for me, with out legs and one arm once they discover that I was wounded out of pity they would give me ten Gold Stars, while others, think that I was a fool to go to The War and Fight in the first place and there has not been one Asian person that have given me Five Stars since I have been driving for UBER; they still have regrets from losing the wars in Japan, Viet-Nam, Korea and all those other countries where The Imperialistic Regime came into to those impoverish nations and used their Democratic Tactics and divided their whole country-so just think about that"

Oh My God-it is like that Mitch"

"Yes, UBER is Psycho-social, UBER is Political for the Drivers, UBER is opinionated and UBER is 'EARTH ITSELF IN A ROLLING MOVING BALL OF FIRE TAKING PEOPLE FROM HERE TO THEIR, JUST AS THE EARTH MOVES, SO DOES UBER"

"Wow, I never thought about it like that-so what your saying is, UBER is WORLDLY and you have got to be Political, Social and have a Great attitude and accept anything and everything that opens the door to your car"?

"Yes, you catch on quick, don't you"?

"Well let's move Mitch and thanks for the UBER Lesson" I had no idea that UBER, is more than just a MOBILE, HIGH TECHNICAL TRANSPORATION SYSTEM, UBER IS A SCIENCE, NOT YET DISCOVERED BY THE SCIENTIST THEMSELVES?

"Let's roll, we got a Pool Hit on the system"

Chapter XXIV

Pooling the Movers
of Uber!

UBER Madness, why Mitch is completely insane when it comes to driving for UBER-I have never seen such a drastic change in one's personality as when Mr. Mitchell got into this Black Malibu, Chevrolet with all Black tinted windows, flipped on the ON STAR system and suggested that Jimi Hendrix, Machine Gun, be played, by his voice tone.

"This is a mad machine Mitch," I said.

"Buckle up and prepare for transport"

"What-why you take your job very serious, don't you"

"Why yes, but not only that, there is a warning signal blinking on my dash indicating that I will not be able to move until you place your seat belt on"

"Boy am I in for a ride…" we took off like a bat out of hell, once my seat belt was snapped, so did Mitchell brain snap.

"What's that you got their Mitch, playing some Hendricks"

"Yes sir, don't need coffee in this mission once I played some Hendricks"

"What was that, can you turn the music down a little, I can't here you" The music of Hendricks guitar was so load I could barely hear him talking. What a performer this Mitch fellow is-a natural born Mover/GROOVER of the UBERS.

"Now, there she is, you just say hello and be professional-now, your M O is an attorney going to Century City, to your office-this girl, according to her manifest is going to Venice Beach to work, most likely-they try to save as much money as possible by ordering a pool ride where they will split the fare with you Synder"

"But I do not have a UBER Account"

"You don't need one, you are with THE UBER GROOVER TODAY"

"How you know that is the rider" I asked Mitch.

"You see, she's looking at her cell phone, she is following me as I make my approach-closer, closer, now, you see how she just looked up from watching her cell phone, she knows her ride is here-change sides on the seat so I can scope her up-remember, be gentle" Snyder, wow, he is a true driver, I thought to myself.

"How are you maim, I am your UBER Driver-am I correct, your name is Hazel and you selected the Pool" Mitch said so eloquently and professionally, knowing, that he had three ladies of the night in his room until 9 a.m. he sure was gentlemanly toward his new client.

"Yes, that is correct, my name is Hazel and your name is Mitchell, Mitchell Martinez"? The young lady said, as I was impressed with the instant contact that Mitch made, good voice mannerism, good eye contact and a good representation of the company that he drives for.

"Please have a seat Hazel and there is some chocolates and mints in the center divider and there is a chilled bottle of Perrier water-please let me know if you have enough leg room maim or Hazel"? By the way, this gentleman is a attorney that works in Century City, his name is Synder and he will be sharing the ride with you"

"Oh, hye Mr. Synder, what type of attorney are you"?

"Criminal Maim, I am a criminal attorney," I said criminal, since it is really a crime that what Mitch is perpetrating for a five star rating; he is a complete gentleman though.

"Have you had any tough cases lately" Hazel asked.

"Oh, I am still interning but we did handle such cases as Chris Brown and his assault on Rhiannon"

"Wow" said Hazel and then Mitch intervene as we were instructed to drive toward Venice on the GOOGLE Application.

"We will be taking you to your destination first Hazel, since the traffic is flowing and, can I ask, what time do you have to be at your destination today" asked Mitch.

"Twelve o'clock"

"Oh, so I made a good choice to take you first and then I will be taking Mr. Synder to his office"

"What a Charmer" I thought to myself as Mitch drove and I sat in my seat and just observed him maneuver the high technical instruments on his steering wheel.

"Beep, Beep, Bing-another call came in the Google application as Mitch interjected that he will not be picking up the passenger, since it will be taking him way out of the way and Hazel may be late for work-now why would a rider choose the POOL, because Hazel would only have to pay three dollars, on the average and Eighty Seven Cent for a five mile drive to her job.

"I am in no hurry today Mitchell, you can pick up the other passenger" I told Mitch.

"Go ahead, I can be a little late-it is okay with me Mitchell" said Hazel.

"Okay-the call is just a block away and chances are the rider will be going to the same area-I will pick up Jessica and then I will drop you off at your work place and then Mr. Synder; everyone agrees"?

"Fine with me" I said.

"No problem" said Hazel.

Once Mitch, took a look at the passenger, knowing that the person he was to pick up is a female and sure enough, looking at her cell phone at the application provided by Google showing Mitch vehicle approaching her.

Mitch speeded up and did not pick up the rider, the young lady waiting on the corner of Washington and Sepulveda, as Hazel and I was surprised and at odds with each other.

"Sorry, I just got a signal from UBER that this client is using a made up Craig's List Account, so I just pressed okay and rejected the pick up" Mitch said.

"She is mad as heck Mitchell"

"Serves her right, that bitch, she is a Puta from the East Side Mongol's and I would beat her ass if she got inside this car"

"What, you mean to tell me that the girl that Mitchell passed on was a gang member and you are a gang member Hazel"

"Yeah, I am a Gang Banger and she is a Banger and we do not like each other," said Hazel as Mitch, laughed it off and proceeded to Venice too drop Hazel off at her restaurant where she waited tables.

"Thank you Hazel and have a good day"

"Good by, drop into my restaurant sometimes and have some food on me Mitchell"

"Will do, now you have a good day," Mitch said as we speed off.

"How did you know Mitch-I mean, I looked at you from behind your head and I knew something was not right and you acted accordingly, real quick"

"And you want to be a UBER Driver-you see Snyder, if you would have looked at the tattoos and the codes on Hazels fingers when she got inside the car with experience, you would have know although she seems like a good young lady, those were gang emblems and the girl on the corner of Sepulveda and Washington with her baggy cloths and her hat turned backwards in red is from another rival gang-those two gangs do not mix-they go to battle with each other-it was a close call"

Mitch was using his UBER Magic and avoided a incident that we would have possibly made the nightly news-those two gals may have been packing guns-what a good call, it is like being in a war zone and knowing that a civilian is carrying a bomb to go off once you drew near-Mitched saved the day.

"Another Hit, this one is in Huntington Beach, you see Snyder, the Google app's indicate that this client sometimes have two other passengers yet she choose to Pool for the discount"

"So, if the client has two, three or four other passengers, what do you do Mitch"

"I press this little button here and it brings down on the phone six chooses and I press the cancel due too MUCH LUGGAGE-of course there are other options but if I want to get paid five dollars for the ride over within the five minutes limit I choose Too Much Luggage"

"That is a shame that you UBER drivers must pay for your own gas, maintenance and insurance and Wi-Fi" I sympathized with Mitch.

"It is a right off, but not for me, you see, the government pays me a pension for the lost of my limbs so it all breaks even on my takes, I am tax exempt but then again, I am not tax exempt when it comes to driving UBER"

"You mean to tell me, you pay for the gas to pick up these people and you pay for the Wi-Fi and insurance and you do not get a penny back" I asked Mitch by looking at the back of his head from the back seat.

"That's right"

"You drive people for free-for a matter of fact, you pay out of your own pocket to drive people you do not even know"!

"Half right-I know them, they are my therapy"

"Your therapy-how so Mitch"

"They got me out of my depression and they talk to me, they have confidence in me and for me, I got to carry out my mission"

"Your mission, why Mitchell, you are not in the Military no longer, you're a civilian and you are in a private industry transportation system, not the Army Corp of Engineers"

"It's all the same, the mission, the promise to deliver, no matter if it is a bomb or a person; the mission must be accomplished"

"Look Mitchell, how long has it been since you visited the Veterans Hospital and talked to a therapist"

"A year or so"

"Well, you have transference"

"Transportation, not transference Snyder"

"No Mitchell, look, I really like you as an individual and I admire your hard work and your compassion for your country and the people you drive but, you have a wife, three triplets and a family that loves you and you can not continue to be transfixed on UBER"

"UBER does have a way to take you into their pool and poison you"

"That is what happens when you get into your car to dive Mitchell, even I noticed the change in your disposition-you flashed back to the time when you transported bombs and chemicals, not people-you got to get more help Mitchell"

"I will, as soon as I make my 2500 rides, I will get help, I will get help real soon Synder-but for now, let me fill you in on these clients-I picked them up before and what they do is go on these Cruise Ships and they mingle with the single men and the business men that leave their wives at home"

"It says all of that on your cell phone application, on Google"

"No, but the name-it says Misty and Stormy; and that it the code for me that Misty, my friend and her friend stormy is taking a trip-they go every other week to the San Pedro Pier and clean up with a few thousand dollars after they return to the port"

"This is a Mobile Whore House that you are running Mitch and I do not want to have any part of it-so you can drop me off back at the hotel" I told Mitch.

"Well, there goes your Pulizer Prize in Journalism"

"What"

"Or maybe, that other one that they give to journalist, The Nobel Prize or maybe, if you get the job done on this enigmatic, mysterious phenomenon that I am showing you, you may get The Queen of England, Night Hood Maybe"

"Mitchell are you cohousing me now"

"Maybe, maybe not; just ride with me to this next client and see for yourself what us UBER drivers, cab drivers, limousine driver and private driver have to go through everyday dealing with people-just this one and I am sure you will be convinced that this is a Phenomenon, not a People's Mover organization"

"Okay, lets go, I am with you-whores or no whores, drug dealers or no drug dealers, Gang Bangers or no Gang Banger, I am with you, let's Move"

Chapter XXV

Transporting, Transvestite

To A
Cruise Event!

"Hello Love" Mitch told the client, as we drove to Huntington Beach to pick up our next passengers-Mitch made certain that the Blue tube was on as I listen to their respond.

"Mitch, if you don't get your Black-_ _ _ over here, what's taking you so long to pick up Dear"

"405, and that is not a cleaning formula, that is the freeway puddin"

"Come on Mitch, we are going to be late for our trip, are you ever going to go with us"

"Who will drive UBER if I go on the Cruise with you two-be there in a few-I have a friend with me"

"Bring it on," said Jennifer, as I thought to myself; what an unusual conversation from the other riders that Mitch picked up. Why he was so casual and down to earth with these gals-he is a hell of a guy that Mitch.

"Now these two are friends that ride UBER on a regular basis Snider; they are taking the cruise ship to Catalina Island and I think you will be happy with their conversation"

"What ever you say Mitch" I agreed and thought to myself, after two days of being with Mitch, nothing would surprise me.

We arrived at a non-entry gate that Mitch had the code and just let himself inside the condominium complex. We drove up and Mitch asked me to take their luggage and place the bags inside the truck of the car.

From the window Mitch said hello and the girls were wearing Floridian attire, very bright with Pascal's and yellows and oranges; they were ready for the cruise during the winter month in California.

"Synder, the spider, this is Jennifer and Julie-this is my friend from England Snyder the old spider"

"Hello love, from England, how nice what part of England Spider Man" said Jennifer and by now, I felt that something was very wrong-why, these were, they are-these people are men dressed in drag-oh my Goodness-I said out load as Mitch, Jennifer who's formally name was Jennie and Julia name was Julius-I was statured but I could put nothing pass Mitch.

"I live in Southern England, Waterloo"

"Oh, we have been there, why you're near the Buckingham Palace and Themes"

"That's right"

"Julia and I just love to watch those changing of the guards and the funny part about it Spider, I told Jennifer told, that we are going to take the tour to see them change the guards and she saw the guards and said: I really want to see them Change those Big Boys Diaper; Diaper, get it Spider Man"

"That one I have heard many time from tourist-so you two have totally changed your gender"

"No, we just feel free as women, not men and we are happy with what we are and enjoy life Spider"

"Well that is understandable-shall we get aboard and proceed" said Mitch, as I put the last suit case inside the truck of the car and Mitch used his cell phone to place the Pick Up on the phone while we took the 405 freeway to San Pedro where the two were to take a cruise to Catalina and then Mexico.

"So, what do you do Snyder the Spider" said Julia, who was wearing so much make up that she could have passed for Bozo the Clown instead of a Gay Old Transvestites.

"Mitch" I called out to get his approval to reveal who I am.

"Sure Snyder, you can be yourself with these gals, they are true friends, one of the best a man could ever have" Mitch said.

"Well, I work for Rolling Stone Publications and I was commissioned to do a story on UBER"

"UBER, well you are at the right place honey; this man here is The UBER GROOVER and he can tell you some stories of his trips that are unbelievable"

"That is what I have gathered already-now, how long have you known The Grover"

"Why we were his first-I mean, his first passengers weren't we sweetie"

"That you were-why, these were the two that taught me how to use the function and when I use to drive, or can I say, when I use to commandeer the Google Self driven car, they are the one's that showed me how to win over my clients with style and class" said Mitch, The Groover.

"Do you UBER often"

"Not as much as we would like since we had a bad experience with a UBER driver that refused to transport us since we are different-baby, we just called Mitchell and he was here in a flash and once that other UBER driver saw The King of The UBER's Mitch, he started bowing and apologized too us and oh, it was just pitiful weren't we precious" said Jennifer to Julia.

"Yes, one of our worst experience with UBER that I do not think we can ever live down" said Julia.

"So Mitch, how is it, that you command the other drivers and you are designated as The King of UBER, The UBER GROOVER"

"Simple, I went in their and got a team of attorneys too fight for all the UBER drivers benefits and back pay and gas and maintenance that was spent over the years-I risked my own job and my family security to fight for all the UBER Drivers and guess what, we won the biggest Class Action Suit in the history of California"

"Not only that, just look at him, isn't he the the most handsome and charming man that you have ever encountered'

"That he is, that he is truly is-one of a kind that Mitchell Martinez is, a good fellow" that's all I could say, and what a trip all the way from Huntington Beach to San Pedro with Mitch, Jennifer and Julie, and the information that I got from the gals will put me on top of the list of all time Journalism stories and I owe it all to Mitch.

"Now that we dropped them off, who were they or should I say, what were they Mitch"

"People, just like you and me, but one thing you have got to understand and put into your book, your magazine or whatever and where ever you take this experience; people are moving, from one destination to another with all the technology and UBER, it is cost effective and fast for them to get from point A to point B Snyder"

"But can't you see what UBER has done, can't anyone see that UBER has made the Yellow Cab, the oldest and most efficient mode of transportation in it's day, go out of business; the municipal bus services in cities are at a deficient and on the verge of places hundreds of old and brand new buses in parking lots just sitting there because UBER is used extensively-even the electric rail system is out of millions of dollars and the tax payer will have to make up the deference since no one rides those services anymore" I told Mitch emphatically.

"Well, they had years to up date their system with Google and the other technical application but they horded all their profits that they made from innocent people that they ripped off-so, Karma is something else' 'isn't' it Snyder.

"No public utility service can compete with UBER"

"Yeah, and look at this on my cell phone; the pay out just got accumulated and all the way from Huntington Beach, California to San Pedro, Eleven Dollars and Eighty Seven Cent-now you tell me if that is not the greatest deal you ever heard of?"

"Dammit-that is a deal, why that is over twenty miles, one way, how do they do it Mitch, I mean, how does UBER charge so less for so much comfort, service and professional 24 hours a day, any day of the week Moving People all over the entire world"

"Exploit"

"Exploit-what do you mean Mitch"

"Oh, your English, you know what I mean since your people were so good at it when they went over to Africa and just took Two Million Africans from their villages and their families and their culture and in-slaved them into dehumanized animals; now that is Exploitation and that has come back on you English 10 folds each and every time the Sun and the moon rotates in their cycle"

"Your crazy, why I did not have anything to do with that-it was people that were high up in the British Hierarchy Mitch, you can not put that one on me after four hundred years ago"?

"No-if I was free, I would not be a dam UBER Driver"

"You told me that the government pays you five thousand dollars per month in pensions and you get free medication and you can get free housing and you took the UBER job because you wanted to work"

"So did the Slaves"

"So did the slaves what-what now Mitch"?

"The slaves, those people that have the same DNA as me, that your people kidnapped and brought over in slave ships and sold-UBER is no better that a slave trader on Mobile Wheels"

"Oh, come on now Mitch-you better take some of your medicine-I tell you what, you can take me back to the hotel, I am out, I have had enough of this UBER thing"

"Sure, get in, but congratulations, you have a great story now-you have meant the real people that ride UBER, you have made contact with how the streets use the technological Google to direct and move UBER passengers, you got it all Snyder and it will make a Great Story, you even meant Transvestites that would die if UBER is taken from them-but you have not gone into Compton and Watts; I mean the Hood to see how the other UBER Passengers live with UBER Movers"

"Watts, Compton, well how far is that from San Pedro"?

"Right across the bridge, I can take a right hook and the 110 freeway and have you there in no time then, take you to the Hotel-I will have to turn off the Google system until we get there because we do not want to pick up those fancy, pansy riders, going to the airport and those college students going to class this time of morning, do we Snyder"

"Very well, since it is on the way to the hotel, besides, I have enough material to write a novel"

"So, what will you call the novel Snyder"?

"UBER-GROOVER/MOVERS, of course"

"Well Called-now, let's UBER it to Compton"

Chapter XXVI

Uberhood

It was getting late in the afternoon by now. Mitch drove the Malibu, too which he called: Bu, as if it was his gal. It was plain to see and hear that he was still fighting the war-he thinks he is still back in Iraq or Afghanistan, in his training and in his awareness of the passenger that he "Labels" he can call it like it is, the females, the dope dealers that use UBER for their drops and pick ups. The prostitutes that he calls them "HIS PEOPLE" The sociologist and Psychologist would call this type of behavior: Cognitive Recognition and Transference, since the people that he acquainted his self with are used to protect himself. Mitch gains friends for his own personal attributes. Word moves fast in the UBER Social Circle and Mitch is the godfather of all the Uberist Culture.

"We are just about there in the area, you see, once we make the transition from the Harbor Freeway to the 105 Century Freeway, going east we have placed ourselves in the HOOD, Watts, Compton, so all I got to do is press the UBER LOGO button and you see Snyder, already a Bing"

"Wow, that was quick-they really need drivers in this area right Mitch"

"Not really, no UBER driver wants to go to this side of town-there has been many of drivers killed and beaten up and robbed in this side of town"

"So why are we going into the killing zone"

"You got to look at all facets of the UBER territory, not just the good areas-you see Snyder-these same UBER riders take their rides to Beverly Hills, Torrance, Santa Monica and other area to rob, terrorize and they make their living off being transported by The UBER Apps"

"Can't they do a character check on the riders Mitch"?

"You can buy a UBER Credit account on Craig's list, so the criminals too use UBER for their basic needs of survival just like all the other people that use UBER to get to work, to school and to their recreation needs, some of these people use UBER to Rob and kill"

"Oh my"

"Don't get Squamish Snyder; now, you see on this trip; it says to make sure you check how many passengers and there is a whole list; 1,2 and 3 riders have tried to use the one person that is really registered for the ride, so UBER is notifying me to be careful"

"You're the security for UBER too"

"A UBER driver is everything and everywhere Snyder-we run these cities and the people love us-did you see when that Neurosurgeon beat up the UBER driver and the repercussions that happened when all the people that ride UBER called in and threatened the life of that Doctor"

"Yeah, I saw that on Google, that little girl kicked the UBER driver right in the balls"

"We get a lot of that-and do you still want to drive for UBER"

"Hell No"

"Calm down and once you leave this area, you can make your own decision on driving-I can get you in as a driver real quick, but first-Check Out The Bottom and tell me what you think about UBERING-it"

"Take a Look-there are the passengers on the pool list, those bags are cloths and it indicates that they are being Evicted or there is a domestic dispute, now, I think that I am going to switch up and let you take the drivers wheel and see if you pass the test of UBERING-IT"

"Really, you're going to let me handle the riders"

"Sure, go for it, I got to tighten up my prosthetics and now, make the switch-take the realm Snyder, you are me now" Wow, in the short time that I have been involved in documentary journalism I have never been directly involved in a real life event-this should be exciting.

"Go for it-you UBERETE" said Mitch, who had a nickname for everything that is done in his UBER LIFE.

"UBER MAIM" I asked the rider whom appeared to be in her pajama's wearing a headscarf, carrying a baby on her hip.

"You the UBER Man Mitchell-that is what is on my cell phone but you don't look like you Black on my cell phone" Ashika, the name on the manifest said as I came up with the lie.

"Oh, I am in training and Mr. Mitchell, your regular UBER DRIVER is training me maim; so, how many bags do you have"

"Oh, I have a few more bags, here, hold the baby while I go get the other bags, it will not be long-thank you, the baby like you"

"Why sure maim, but do you have a car seat-I can not legally drive a baby without a car seat"

"Yeah, I will bring it out with the bags-now, just give me a minute and I will get the bags and we can get out of here, fast" Aisha said.

"Where and the hell do you think your going with my Bitch White Boy" said a Big Bully Black Man with muscles from shoulder to shoulder that literally scared the living shit out of me.

"UBER, sir" I said, as the gal jumped all in the front of me and the BIG BULLY BLACK MAN, that was mad as Hell"

"I did not order a Uber, and this Bitch isn't going nowhere with my son; so get back in the house Bitch and give me my son mother F'er"

"Why sir, I am just a UBER driver and I was called to pick up the young lady, you need not get all railed up and angry" "What you say White Boy" said The Big Bully Black Man.

The gal to whom I was to pick up got right into the mix and between the Big Black Man that I assumed is her husband or boyfriend, while the Black Man thought that I was intruding on his female companion and from his back pocket he pulled out a gun.

"Oh, don't kill me, I am with UBER, I don't want to die," I cried out.

"Hold it my Nigger, now put the gun down, right now and take your Bitch and those black trash bags into your shack and that sticky ass baby" Why it was Mitch, holding a 357 Magnum Gun, with the longest barrel that I have ever seen in my life, pointing right at the head of The Black Man.

"Hold on Homey, this white man is trying to take my girl and baby off somewhere," he said.

"We are UBER and she called us to pick her up, what is being indicated here homeboy; you mean to tell me that your straggling ass bitch did not tell you that she is leaving you, getting away-did you two have a fight" Mitch said, as I could feel the piss rolling down my leg on the dead grass right here in a place that I did not want to die; Compton, California.

"That's your business, now, I am only going to tell you one more time, get the gun off my friend and handle your own business homey-we can settle this right here and have the Ground Hog deliver your mail or we can sit down inside your home at the conference table and you two can talk about your disputes-that little boy is going to be looking for his daddy when he get's of age and the momma is going to say he died right here on the front lawn by a UBER DRIVER, now, take that 22 bee-bee gun from my buddy head and we can talk about this inside"

Mitch saved my life as the Big Black Man stood down as the rider Aisha, The Big Black Man and Mitch, went into the little wooden house and the couple argued for a few minutes and then, with in a half of an hour, believe it or not, the Big Black man, the Baby and Aisha came out of the house holding each other; I could not believe what just happened. The Life and Times of a UBER Driver.

"Mitch, what just happened?" I asked Mitch as he jumped back into the car on the driver's side and said good-bye to Aisha, the Black Man and the little boy Bryan.

"This is UBER my man and these are the streets that we Move People to places, now, my only question is are you in or are you out as a UBER Partner Driver"

"If I can just go somewhere and change out of these wet pants-I really got to think about it Mitch-what just happened, where did that 357 magnum come from"

"I got a permit, a license, Snyder, I do security too on some celebrity riders"

"Thank God-I was almost killed"

"By a toy gun-that Nig was holding a toy pop gun Snyder, you got to pay attention hommie are you will die in these streets and in Braxton, England when you return home as a so called Journalist" We drove on.

"Where are we going now Mitchell"?

"Over some of my UBER GROOVER BUDDIES right here in Compton; you will get the UBER EPIC Stories from these Old Timers that pull in One thousand dollars a week driving UBER, they trained me Snyder"

"Can I change my pants there"?

"Yes, I have some extra pants in the trunk of the car, your just about my size-sure, you can shower up and change over their house" said Mitch as we turned on a few corners and we pulled up on the front lawn of their house.

Chapter XXVII

Old Gangster (O G's)

UBER'G'S.

It was only a quarter of a mile away, when we turned into the front lawn that was dirty brown and a house that was painted in pink with rusted shutters and security bars all on the windows. A scene of the movie: Training Day, one of my favorites that us Brit's enjoyed the scenery and the unsuspectingly candid behaviorism of the Los Angeles Police Department Detective; whom Denzel Washington played the role of a crooked cop, under pressure, went to the wrong side of justice.

At the door where, since I was gaining the gift of observance; the one thing, that I did discover through my brain and through the inherited gift to survive; the fight or flight syndrome, that Mitch taught me, to always be aware of your immediate environment.

"Hit that door bell Snyder" I pressed the door ring, while Mitch, adjusted his prostatic legs.

"Yeah" the voice from the door, while it was still closed rung out, as I still continued to gaze at the yard and all the vehicles parked on the grass and the sidewalk toward the garage.

"GROOVER-it's me-open the door my Nig" What the Nig meant is the hyphenated word for Nigger that I noticed in my time with Mitch, he always criticized the Japanese for not giving him his five star rating; Mitch always talked about the Hispanics and them laying forts in his back seat, as he put it, those chili beans that they eat; and he always talked about The White people being of Colonial descent only to use those privileges to exploit other cultures and enslave them. What a piece of work that Mitchell.

The wooden door opened and then the screen door as the young African American Man peeped and looked at me, up and down and then, once he looked at The GROOVER, he got all the acceptance that was necessary for us to enter, as if he was of Royalty.

"Mitch, what brings you too this side of town" the young man said.

"Oh, just perusing the Hood"

"Who is this White Boy your with, one of your passengers"

"No, he is from Rolling Stones Magazine and this is Snyder and he's doing a interview of that Class Action Settlement that we won and he want to see how it's like to drive for UBER" Mitch told the young man who's name was Jason.

"Where's Todd"

"He's coming; he had a bad night last night driving UBER" said Jason.

"I tell you, those night runs will get you all the time-why you think your picking up a legitimate passenger, an attorney, a doctor or a executive from Taco Bell and you could be picking up The Devil"

"I like the night life GROOVER-I get to kick it with the ladies"

"Watch out for them too, why they will get you all crossed up little homie and then, UBER will have a major Law Suit that the bitch files for you rapping her in a UBER vehicle"

"UBER pays out though GROOVER"

"With sixty eight billion in their accounts they did pay out but those days are over my friend, why the company will have to pay us out over Two Hundred and Eighty Seven Million Dollars in back pay, and that is only in the United States alone"

"Thanks a lot GROOVER, for taking the case to the level that you did"

"Don't thank me my Little Nig, thank Todd and all the Old Timers that schooled me on how UBER uses and exploits their drivers; why if it were not for Todd and the rest of the UBER GROOVER GANG, I would be still out there struggling and asking questions about; they hipped me to what was really going on and how we were exploited like Slaves on a Plantation Farm"

"How long you been driving Jason"

"Do you know me?" said Jason to Snyder.

"Jason, it is okay, he's from the magazine that I told Todd about, you can answer his questions; I got Todd's approval" said Mitch, and right then and there I knew that UBER was a Hierarchy of Drivers that controlled the hundreds of thousand of other drivers; why UBER would not protect the drivers, against The Yellow Cab destruction of the UBER drivers personal vehicles when their vehicles got egged and the windows broken out. UBER was not going to protect the drivers from lawsuits unless it could be proven through a camera that the technology failed and that the drivers were right and forthcoming. UBER never even answers their phone line and their email when it comes to the driver's needs and complaints-they had to form a committee, a protection source, a UBER GANG called THE GROOVER, of UBER.

"Somebody called my name"

"Todd, what happening big fellow"

"Mitch-what the hell took you so long to stop by here and see your boy" said Todd-a fair skinned brother with, what looked like a deformity with his left hand, a birth defect from what I could see.

"They suspended me since I organized to take them to court on that Class Action Suit when they where taking all the Disabled Veterans Pension; why we had to take a stand in court and we one my Nig"

"We sure did, but I heard that they will appeal the multi-million dollar pay out Mitch"

"No, they will settle, but there will be some changes around here-we will get benefits, more pay, more gas and maintenance for our cars and those riders, God Bless Their Hearts, will be paying three time the amount to ride with UBER"

"Karma-they were always getting a free ride on the salary of us drivers, Mitch, anyway-who's the dude" said Todd.

"Snyder, he's the one that is doing the interview for Rolling Stones Publications and he thinks that he has enough material to write an entire novel of The Life and Time's of A UBER DRIVER" said Mitch, as I got up from my seat on the coach and waited for my introduction to Mitch's UBER GURU, the UBER driver that made Mitch the man he is today as a driver. I shook his hand.

"Your not from these parts of the Hood are you Snyder" said Todd.

"I am from the mother country Mr. Todd, England, Great Britain"

"Yeah, I can tell, why while Mitch has one thousand passengers on his passenger list of riders, I have over two thousand riders from all over the world-say Mitch, have you taken Snyder to Beverly Hills where all your High Price Gals Work"

"Oh yeah, we did that and been there with them-he was startled"

"How about The Show Girls, the stripper Trips"

"That would be a little too much for Snyder, he has got to acquire a few more skills to be able to go down that road T"

"Why, what's wrong; why earlier you said I graduated from UBER 101 Mitchell and there is more to be learned"

"Snyder, this is a Cult, a Brain Washing, high phonetically high pollutant, exploitive organization and it will take more time for you to gain your Five Stars with UBER"

"My mind is made up, since I had that last incident-I want the High Life of a UBER Driver Mitch"

"No, you got to get back to The Mother Country and submit that article and when and if you ever return, then, you can be a UBER GROOVER"

"Yeah my British Homey, you got to finish that article and then, come back and see your boy Mitch and The GROOVER'S why there are a few hundreds of us and we protect ourselves from those that are trying to infiltrate our system, our pay, our turf and our families-now, how long will it take you to finish the magazine article"?

"Two to three months" I told T for Todd.

"Good, not let me school you, like my homey Mitch schooled you look out there, in the yard, now you tell me, what do you see"

"Well, I see a lot of dead grass and steal fence and four Prism, Toyota cars"

"Good, Mitch, I can tell you have taught Snyder the first rule of surviving UBER-observation and survival in your immediate environment-good-but do you know or have any idea what those vehicle's cost us-those are lease cars that UBER own and they are only rented too us for Three Hundred and Eighty Seven Dollars a Week, now tell me, is that exploitation or can I say aspiration"

"That's exploitation, wow, how can you all afford three hundred and eighty seven dollars a week, how can your crew afford that kind of payment each week"

"We can't, why we work all night and all day, picking up each and every passenger that we can, sometimes over eighteen passengers a day and since they reduced the riders payments to UBER by fifteen to twenty percent less in pay, we can't make payments on our only means of transportation-can you help us"

"Yes, I can, and I will; you got a computer so I can email my office in England"

"Why, sure, right back there in my room-don't worry, the pit will not bite you, hear, let me show you where the computer is; all the other driver are sleep, we had a hard night last night"

"You mean to tell me that this house is where you all board yourself and live; you all use this house as a rest home"

"Yes, this is where we rest and shower up and rotate driver, just like the Greyhound bus station, we are always on the move, twenty-four seven, all day and all night seven days a week" said Todd, unbelievable!

After sending the company the first draft they looked forward to the completion so I asked for an additional $10,000.00 ten thousand dollars for additional resources to complete my mission, my project my story on the greatest Exploitation Scheme since Slavery in The United States of America. The director wired me the funds immediately and told me the presses are about to role out: THE UBER/GROOVER: LIFE STYLE OF A TRANSPORATION MOVER OF PEOPLE.

"Is there a U S Bank in the area where I might receive wired funds" I asked Mitch and Todd and looked at Jason's the young UBER driver eyes went wide open with hearing that funds will be sent for information on the Biggest Story of the Century for England since The Grim Sleeper Story that the Australian team of Documetarians filmed in South Central.

"Ten thousand dollars will go to a fund to pay for some of your accounts on those Prism, Toyota Todd" I told Todd and then, the party began as if these gentlemen have just been liberated from Slavery, they grabbed me and it was such a joyous feeling that it was indescribable"

There were tears, there was yelling, there was an immediate of the shackle and chains being released from the angles and the hands of these humans who got into the ship of UBER not really knowing where they were to be sent, not knowing where they would make and how they would pay, out of their own pockets, to an organization a company that made Seventy Billion Dollars and refuse to share with their Partners, the Driver.

"They are throwing you a big party at the Marriott in Carson City Snyder for your help and candid work that you observed of how UBER Is The Worst USER, Ever, since Slavery of Man-Kind" said Mitch, well, after taking that hot shower and going to the bank and retrieving the money and giving it to your UBER GURU, I feel Honored, to have helped"

"Thank you, these guys really need the money to pay off their debt to UBER" said Mitch

"Retribution for a time that the Brit's did have a lot to do with the Slave trade, the Mexican revolution that the Brit's supplied the weapons and the total exploitation of the minority people throughout the world-yes, I did know and understand what you were telling me about the Slave Ships and How The British, made friends with the African natives, only to kidnap them, throw them into Big Slave Ships and selling them, your people all over the world-I know what happened, I researched it" I told Mitch and the young UBER driver that just listened too me and started crying.

Chapter XXVIII

Karma vs. UBER

Mr. Herman Edward Synder had an eventful going away party at the Marriott in Carson, California. Once the news spreader like wild fire that Snyder's group sent the UBER GROOVERS GANG Ten Thousand Dollars, due to the lease contract on their Prism, Toyota that UBER, automatically takes out of their pay check three hundred and eighty seven dollars a week, leaving those drivers at UBERS Began' Call to drive more and more in order not to have their vehicle repossessed. I saw through what UBER can do to a individual when the company tried to take my Malibu from me, but I showed them the Pink Slip that I personally paid the remaining amount to General Motors despite what the Federal Government insisted that the vehicle was all mine for The Veterans Rehabilitation Program.

"Have a safe trip back to England Snyder"

"I will be in contact with you Mitchell and I will make sure that the UBER GROOVER"S get their residuals from the sells of the magazine about UBER" "Thank Mitchell, and you do not know how much I enjoyed my three days with you and documenting the UBER Runs"

"No one would have believed me if I told them that UBER treats their partners like slaves; shackled and chained down by their constantly demanding us drivers to drive, to make your ten quoata, drive to get 15% off on the gas that you buy, drive to get rewards; why the Department of

Transportation would close UBER down if they knew that the UBER Drivers are behind the wheel over fourteen hours per day" I told Snyder.

"Mr. Snyder, you have another interview of a UBER passenger that had a very bad experience with a UBER driver" Snyder was busy. Once the thousands upon thousands of community people found out that the Uber stands for Slavery his company gave The UBER-GROVER's ten thousand dollars for their story on how UBER cheated them on their lease car; hundreds of people lined up to tell their story, good things about UBER and some gruesome things about UBER, Mr. Snyder documented and recorded every one of their stories for his article and maybe his book about UBERING.

Gearing up to drive again from the Marriott in CARSON CITY, to West Hollywood tonight to make up the time that I lost for the three days while showing Snyder the inside outs about UBER.

"Come On Bu (Malibu), your all loaded up with mints, Pierre water and a full tank of gas to ride the night away picking up riders some that will enjoy me and the comfort that they will have in the back seat of a Luxury Malibu, while others will say that this vehicle and I are to fixed up and they will feel intimidated-oh well, the old saying goes that you can please some of the people some of the time but not all of the people all of the time; so true, come on 'Bu, let me put some Tu-Pac on the audio; Sari, play Tu-Pac, the Rider please....

"Tu-Pac, The Rider coming up, enjoy your ride"

"Why thank you-oh, Mr. Snyder left his papers in the back seat of 'BU, a envelope, wait a minute, it has my name on it and says, Mr. Mitchell Martinez, thank you, for the good time; enjoy yourself and for a matter of fact, take a Cruise with OUR GIRLS from Huntington Beach-oh my, it has hundred dollar bills inside. That Snider the Spider has done it again; there must be twenty-five hundred dollars inside this envelop, what a guy, a good guy that I had a lots of fun with over the last three days....

"Blue tube is ringing, it is a call from my wife"

"Baby, when you coming home" said Sylvia.

"Just finishing the interview with Rolling Stone, so I will be on the next flight back to Atlanta baby"

"The babies just took their first steps; I sent you a Video on your phone"

"You did, I must have missed it-I will check it out once I finish my last run for the night"

"Mitch, what happened with the law suit, I mean, the Class Action Law suit against UBER and did that writer get enough material from you to write a article for his magazine"?

"Oh man, I will have to give you the low down on all that happened over the last three days-it was like a Movie Scene out of that movie that Denzel Washington played the crocked cop; I played the role of the Tour Guide for the UBER/Movers"

"That's one of your all time favorite movies-is everything all right-I mean, did you get paid for the interview"

"Yeah, Mr. Snider, the journalist, gave me Twenty five Hundred dollars that I just deposited into our U S Bank account, the entire cash pay out and The Rolling Stone Publishers gave The OLD UBER GROOVER's Ten Thousand Dollars to pay for their leases on their Prius, Toyota's that UBER has Ripped them off with that three hundred and eighty seven dollars a week lease payment agreement" I told Sylvia, my wife and one thing that I made a vow with her, too tell her everything; no matter what; because if you are in the type of business that I am in, she got to know who I am with and who I am driving and everything-UBER did not give a dam if some mad man or mad women would jump in the back seat of my car and slice my throat from ear to ear-my wife had to know everything, even the women that I indulge myself with.

"I look The Rolling Stone Magazine up on Google and did you know that MR. Snyder is the son of the original owners of The Rolling Stone Magazine and other Publications Companies in England"

"Really, well, that explains a lot-Snyder had us posted up in the most luxurious hotel in Beverly Hills and some of your old gang came to the Hotel and gave him an interview"

"Oh, really, it must have been Jessica, Cynthia, and Julie, they called me and told me that they will be working the Beverly Hills area and that they wanted to get out of the business of being an Escort and possibly come visit us in Atlanta and start a new career"

"Those are my girls and they are your good friends and they are always welcomed especially since they are trying to change their careers"

"I heard the street of Los Angeles has gotten worst and that UBER is being used as a High Profile Mobil Hook Up company and there has been some murders of the UBER LOGO in Gang Violence"

"Yeah, it takes all kinds, and UBER need to step up, it's business practices and stop giving rides to dead beats and gang members"

"I just made reservations for you too come home on tomorrows Delta Flight coming right into Atlanta; at night so we will be waiting for you at the airport"

"Okay baby-I am going to make a few runs tonight and then I am going back to the Elyse Hotel on the expense account of The Rolling Stones Magazine"

"Be careful honey-the babies miss you and so do I"

"See you tomorrow evening" I hated to hang up on my wife and she is the best thing that ever happened to me and all that I had to do is be truthful with her and send her the money on the escapade's that I get involved in-that makes her happy and it takes care of that five acre home that we bought in Atlanta.

I hated when I had to leave my family, but I got to make it the best way I know how and whether it is UBER or a private limousine service-the money has to continue to flow. With three kids and a wife, I have responsibility that must be addressed and although UBER is in my opinion a Mobil Transportation Sweat Shop- Uber does give me the space and time I need to spend with my family. I can literally turn off my UBER Application on my cell phone for months, go back to the system and work as long as I want to and then go back to work when I need some extra funds.

The streets of Los Angeles are settled and calm like the sea after the storm this time of night. Sure, I get a few intoxicators who are smart and need a ride home and I am willing to ablidge. The real reason that I am still driving for UBER can only be explained as a Physiological and Psychological purpose; the CHASE OF THE GAME!

The Chase of The Game has implications of the past historic value. What I mean that when man was in the

Neanderthal Period, he had to hunt, to wonder to find and to travel and explore. UBER let's me have those privileges-I can drive and wonder all though Los Angeles to San Francisco, California, picking up people with all types of backgrounds. The people that I pick up as riders will volunteer their stories and with over a thousand passengers under my watch, I can pen point where they originated from whether it is Switzerland or Australia or any and every part of the entire world-I can tell from their dialog and I tell them-You must be from France or Italy or Nigeria-I am usually correct. I read and listen to TAPES ON BOOK for twenty years at the Veterans Hospital and I had a keen ear on the Linguistics of people all over the entire world dialogue- I got at it and that acquired skills each and every time I get into my vehicle and pick up someone from another country. Oh what a joy to conversation with people all over the world driving UBER.

"Beep…Beep…Beep…" Eleven o'clock at night, it must be passengers that are Bar Hoping. Well, if I could have done it, I would. Looking at the destination to pick up the rider, it wasn't no Pool and it wasn't no Ghetto Dwellers are someone looking for a Cheap Ride at my expense; it was the Country Club, near Beverly Hills; The Hidden Hill near the place where Michael Jackson succumbed to his death by a doctor that was greedy and only wanted monetary rewards instead of his professional integrity. Oh well, let me go and pick this client up and it will be the last for the night.

The camera's caught my vehicle and the gates flung open automatically to my total surprise. I was not expecting to be greeted and the security to open the gates without me identifying myself. I guess the security took a look at The UBER sign and that was my passage to enter. What a set up, as I drove through the court yard toward the residence and the only indication of whom I was too pick up, the name, was RTC. the same initials as the accounting firm that cuts my check every Wednesday, on time, every time, with a direct deposit straight into my account. Something seems suspicious, a company with the same initials, with this multi-million dollar mansion, wanting me to pick them up at this time of night. I was on guard for everything and anything at this point as I drove around the stone circle driveway and a man that I assumed was the house servant opened the double doors and as I addressed myself:

"UBER, Sir, I am your UBER Driver" The man, wearing what it appears to be a dinner jacket and a white bow tie, as if he was dressed for a formal occasion.

"Come right on in Mr. Mitchell Martinez; Mr. Synod is expecting you" the Butler or what ever they call themselves these days said.

"I am here for a pick-up, but the name on my cell phone application read: RTC."

"Yes, Mr. Martinez, you are in the right place, Mr. Synod is expecting you right inside the Gallery; The Library" The House Man said.

"Nice place-how many cars can you get in that garage over there"

"Twenty-one Sir"

"Really-what types of cars are in the garage, if you do not mind me asking"

"Ferrari, Bentley Phampton Rolls Royce and The Phamton Rolls Royce-just to name a few, the servant said, as I continued to walk down this long hall with chandeliers that looked like diamonds-now with all those cars and a chaffier driver or servant, why would this Mr. Sandal fellow need a UBER driver, I wondered.

"Mr. Martinez, this is Mr. Sandol" said the Door Man, as I looked and right away, I knew the face of this man-it was THE CEO of UBER, the developer, the creator of the Multi-Billion Dollar Transportation Conglomerate that nearly drove every transportation company out of business with the No-Trills and Low Cost Transportation System.

"Mr. Martinez, it is a pleasure to meet you" He said, wearing a black collar dinner jacket and blue, Chinese emblems throughout his jacket; very fine silk and very impressive, but what the hell did he want with me"?

"Mr. Synod, how are you" I shook my bosses hand and we just looked at each other in amazement; me, a driver of UBER and he, the multi-billionaire that created a company in 2007 that totally surprised the entire world with the new transportation applications from Google that can pin point a driver and map their destination any where in the entire world.

"I do not understand Mr. Synod; what privilege do I have meeting your acquaintances tonight"

"You're the top driver of all The UBER Drivers Mr. Martinez and I would like to invite you to our main office in San Francisco for a ceremony and awards banquet" said MR. Synod, the CEO of UBER.

"Why thank you, Mr. Synod" I knew that there was a catch to it, because if it sounds to good to be true, chances are it is too good to be true.

"But first things are first; you had a interview with The Rolling Stones Publications from England, did you not"

"Well-I can't say I did and I can not say I did not Mr. Synod"

"Maybe this film will refresh your memory of you and a Mr. Snyder, the journalist and patriotic successor of whom his family owns the magazine has furnished us-take a look at the film on the screen that is coming down Mr. Martinez" Why that son-of-a-bitch; that Snyder it is no wonder that he is referred to "AS A SPIDER" a Snitch and Two Timing Trickster; Snider the Spider turned me in and set me up.

"You see Mr. Martinez, it has cost me a great deal of money to get these tapes on your interview with Mr. Snyder and you humiliating and bringing down my company that I founded"

"Well, it is true"

"True, why you completely fabricated the entire ethic and mission of UBER Transportation and after losing a multi-million dollar class action law suit, with the State of California and Oregon, now I am faced with public and private humiliation that I treat the partner-drivers like slaves"

"More like Chauffeur Mobile Sweat Shop Servants-you see Mr. S., when I take a rider three to five miles in my personal car and I pay for the gas and I pay for the Wi-Fi and I pay for the maintenance, for only Three Dollars and Eighty-Seven Cent; that is what you call a Mobile Sweat Shop on Wheels"

"You had nothing when my company recruited you two years ago from the ravish of the war where you lost your ligaments, your arm and your two legs; well guess who paid for those Plastic Prosthetics Mr. Martinez-UBER on the Federal Government Rehabilitation Program"

"Have your House Boy fetch me a chair to sit on and you can have these plastic legs back and this plastic arm-I do not want them since they are from your Slave Trade Profits S."

"No, you keep them, as long as that Magazine article is not published, the arm, the legs and that check on the table is all your; those lovely and darling little babies can go to college on that handsome amount of money Mr. Martinez and that wife of your that loves to shop at The High End Louie Vuitton Stores and Gucci and that Red Bottom Shoe place Christian Louie Vuitton Store where when she rides that stripper pole all night doing her performance will bring her in a great deal of money and satisfaction, now won't it Mr. Martinez"

"How Much Is The Check" Knowing, that this maniac has been spying on me with that Cell Phone Google Application will Bring another law Suit against him and UBER but I need evidence, so, to make a long story short; I used the computer system and signed a Qau-Pro Bono. (legality) Disclosure, that this money is a settlement for not having the article published on UBER and saying that everything and everybody that was interviewed are actors, make believe and not true; it was all made up…I could not wait to leave, as I was escorted out with a envelope with a check for Ten Million Dollars in my hand-boy is my wife going to be happy; if I can make it out of here alive!....

Soon as the check cleared, I contacted the District Attorney's office in Los Angeles and reported the entire incident. Karma will take you out each and every time. Now that UBER is involved for over two hundred law suits; the yellow cab is suing UBER, The Tax Department is Suing UBER for charging the riders airport fee's when it was against the law and a conflict of interest; there was not one civil entity in the entire world that did not have their hand in UBER's pocket. So what went wrong with UBER? UBER sacrificed its loyal drivers for the non-knowledgeable rider. Each and every rider that I transported when the subject came up: How Do You Like Driving For UBER; I explained to them, I like the passengers but I do not like UBERS Plan-Steal from the Drivers and Give to the Riders, low transportation fee's and they, the riders will return.

Chapter XXIX

Ubercide!

Be careful of what you do in life and how you label your transaction because they may come to haunt you. UBER is defined as: uber- /'oober / combining form, denoting an outstanding or supreme example of a particular kind of thing. 'an uberbabe'

Uber- defined: Mobile-friendly-term with literal meaning of "above" in German. Brought to the mainstream in the early 80's by hardcore American punk…

Uber by Merriam Webster: being a superlative example of its kind or class: super. Uber: to an extreme or excessive degree; super<overcool>extreme, superior, really good.

Uber-ABOVE ALL IN THE WORLD, From German National Anthem Lied der Deutsche, composed by Joseph Haydn in 1797.

Nazis-UBER: ueber alles, has: The stars are fighting for the Teuton race. The Firefly of France Marion Polk Angellotti…

UBER: Deutschland uber Alles-Slavery in the slavenorth. com>columnsuber-alles.

Uber-June 20, 2013-we must define the nature and scope of this struggle, or else it will define. "Right he is.

Profits uber Alles! American Corporations and Hitler/ Global Research-Centre…www.globalresearch.ca>profits-ber-alles…

Knowing now, what I did not know then, that UBER is a term used by The Nazi that meant: Slavery for Profit. That's why and how they got their name and their strategy. By putting one group or class into slavery for a profit, the profiteer will make extraordinary gains, name recognition and have a higher degree of partnership within there peer group and within their Country with their Country men. Hitler used the same technique: UBER, when he designed the Volkswagen that meant The Folks, family car. Uber means to make Slaves out of Humans for a profit.

It is no wonder that Mr. S, the founder of UBER wanted too pay me off once I decided to give Snyder the Spider the information on how the drivers of UBER are treated with low pay and very little wages. I was on one of the strongest and prevalent discoveries since The Atomic Bomb was discovered: UBER practices Neo-Nazi Tactics.

The same mentality is how UBER was set up as a transportation business. Slavery for a Profit, that is how UBER exploits it's drivers and gain momentum with the riders, by pitting one group against the other. Well, I am out of the business for good. When it comes to a mission I am all for it but when it comes to Slavery, keep me out of it. I am transferring my car to my home in Atlanta and resigning for good this time from UBER. Momma did not raise no fool and Mitchell R. Martunez is done trying to please some of the people some of the time but not all of the people all of the time.

The flight back to Atlanta was peaceful as I looked at the landscape of The United States of America, the mountains, the waterways and the buildings and then there was nothing but clouds as the plane took off into the sky. What beauty that has become so tragic in the years of multiple aggressions on minority people by police throughout the country that stood for freedom. Oh well, the only thing that I can do at this point in my life is raise my children well and maybe they will make a change in society.

My wife and sister in law meant me at the airport and I was glad to see them as I hug and hugged my wife and she asked me if everything was okay.

"Mitch, is everything alright"

"Well, just put it this was, I have survived UBER"

"That is the best news I had in a long time-so are you really done with UBER now"? She asked.

"Yes, after two years of meeting the most amazing people and traveling all through California, it is time that I spend quality time with you and the kids"

"Well that is a change-is it because all that money that you transferred into our account Mitch"

"Yes, that too has a great deal to do with it-we are officially retired now baby-I signed off on the article that gives the direct consequences of driving for UBER with the CEO of the transportation company and they do not want me ever even mentioning the name UBER ever again"

"You learned your lesson Mitch and you helped a lot of UBER drivers receive their back pay and benefits and they all admire you for that-come on, the kids are waiting to see you at Mother's house, she fixed your favorite meal for you; Barbeque chicken and macaroni and cheese with baked beans"

"Wow, you see what I have been missing-I am home now and I will not be leaving no time soon"

That night while I was in our newly built home-the house phone rung at one thirty in the morning, we ignored that and then my cell phone rung and I knew that something was going on, something bad.

"Hello, I finally answered at the request of my wife.

"Mitchell, this is Snyder"

"Snyder, what is wrong now, why have you called me so early in the morning"

"Well it is in the evening over here in England, but this news can not wait; say I know that you think that I informed the UBER president about the Rolling Stone Article but it was not me; it came from the Board Members of the magazine, that wanted to get the permission to use some of the patented names"

"Okay, so what does that have to do with me Snyder"?

"There is a big story that I received from the wire on a UBER Driver that drove for your company and committed several Murders"

"Ubercide-well that will make a interesting article, won't it Snyder, but couldn't it wait until tomorrow, I mean a descent hour on our time in the United States-the kids and my wife have woke up now"

"Sorry Mitch, but this can not wait-you see, the murdered lives in Michigan, Kalamazoo and he requested that the UBER person that fought for the UBER drivers meet with him-he admires you so much and he was subjected to so many bad things driving for Uber that he wants to tell his story to you and you only-so will you fly over to Michigan and get the story Mr. Mitchell Martinez"

"Snyder, it is three o'clock in the morning and I just got back from Los Angeles a few days ago; now you say that The Murderer of innocent riders of Uber killed people? I have not heard anything about that on the news, although, they have not hooked up our cable yet in the new home-but, I will take a look at it in the morning on my Lap-Top-now, let me finish out my sleep and I will call you later Snyder"

"There is a great deal of monetary incentives involved Mitchell-the Uber Driver will only see and talk to you, he will not even see an attorney until he see and talk too you first"

"Okay, Snyder, I will take a look at that-you say he killed people while driving his Uber car-were the people that he killed inside the vehicle or were they outside the vehicle when he killed or should I say UBERCIDED them, those poor innocent people"

"It was random-he would pick up Uber passengers and then drive by and kill people with his shot gun and then go pick up other people in the same day"

"Oh, he used Uber as a alibi, that's all, he figured that he would tell the police that the killer was not him since he is a Uber driver and working-sounds interesting but why me Snyder"

"He read all about you during the court hearings on that Class Action Law Suit against Uber and he really got into the case and now, he wants you to get his confession of how Uber made him kill those people"

"You got to be kitting me Snyder, where do you get these lunatics, I tell you what, I will call you in the morning as soon as I take a look at this situation on my Google Media, I will take a hard look at this UBERCIDE, and get right back with you-now you say there is a big incentive for me, to fly all the way to Michigan and have all the cameras and journalist and all of that Publicity that you Snyder and Rolling Stones Magazine Hunger for"

"You got that right Mitch-email me and let me know what will work for you-Rolling Stone Publications got to be on top of this story a.s.a.p. Mitch"

"Okay, I will, it sounds like Truman Capote, The Glass House novel where Truman goes to this little town in the bread basket state, a farm town and interviews a few murderers that committed a crime for, what they thought, was the old farmers money that was hidden in a safe-all of that turned out to be false and the entire family was killed and the Murderers got a Hanging in the Town Square-what a great novel"

"Exactly, and you can do it Mitch-you know uber, you're the Uber GROOVER, the mover and only you can put the pieces together" said Snyder and I hung up on him, until tomorrow.

Chapter XXX

Uberration/Celebration

CASE CLOSED.

Kalamazoo, Michigan; seventy-five miles from Detroit and a once mid-east city that bought thousands of automotive jobs to the city, then, everything collapsed with NAFTA, a Clinton Administration initiative that gave incentives to Mexico and China to built automobiles and parts outside the United States. With my long Leather coat and Pandora brim, I was transported to the city jail system, where Jason, the former Uber driver, is assumed to have killed six people. What was he thinking? What did Uber have to do with his decision, if he did Ubercides, if not, why did Rolling Stones Magazine, assigned me to take a deep look into the case. Rolling Stone Publications, only wanted to profit off the event of the Ubercides. Why didn't they send me to talk to the victim's family instead of talking to the Murderers? All of these questions will be answered once I complete my interview with Jason, The UBERCIDER.

"Mr. Martinez, Jason will see you now, right this way but there is another visitor that will be visiting with Jason and he informed us that he is familiar with your skills and your experience with Uber" said the detective, who prepared me to interview with Jason, the Uber driver.

"Doctor Kagan, I am sure the two of you will cross interview and just remember, you only have one hour per day to talk to Jason, that is all the time he has per day according to the court judge" said the other detective. I had a hard time getting through the screening since I was wearing the plastic legs (prosthetics) but the prosthetics did have screws and bolts that prevented me from interring the security machine.

"Kagan, what are you doing here" I came face to face with my old therapist at The Veterans Medical Center-I was totally surprised that he was here all the way from Los Angeles to interview the inmate that could very well receive the death penalty for the murders of six people.

"For the very same reason you are here Mitchell, to try to get some answers to the gruesome killings of Jason of innocent bystander people" said Doctor Kagan, my previous psychiatrist for the past ten years whom worked with me and got me in the program as a Uber drive through The Federal Government Rehabilitation Program.

"So who sent you, I mean, who informed you of incident"

"The Uber President and CEO"

"Oh, I get it, you are here to interview me, not Jason-what is the meaning of this Doctor Kagan"?

"There is no meaning, as of yet, I just want to have a few minutes with you"

"For what, I have not been retreated with you for at least two years"

"Yes, and that is what give me the authority to be here, it would have been a conflict of interest and against all the protocol of The Psychiatry guidelines for me to otherwise have a moment with you when I am interviewing Jason, the former Uber Driver at the same time"

"We only have an hour so you can ask me anything you want and that does not mean that you will receive an answer"!

"I will try to convince you to not intervene and or interview the client"

"The client, he is not my client, he is just a man that killed six people and I was sent to do a story upon Jason's request"

"What license do you have and you're a Uber driver not a journalist, not a psychiatrist, you're a driver and not a person that can help this man"

"He requested that I see him Kagan, and sure enough, the Uber Corporation want to know everything and anything that is coming from the man's that is assumed to have killed those six people since, I am sure, there will be plenty of law suits coming out of this tragedy"

"Well, you did learn something from being a patient of mine for the past ten years and that is the skills of seeing through the ideology and getting straight to the problem at hand-that is the reason you were my best patient Mr. Mitchell Martinez, I trained you very well and that is the reason you became the top Uber Driver and received that handsome bonus from Mr. S., of over Ten Million Dollars not to disclose any information about Uber"

"That is not the reason I was paid that amount of money"

"So you were paid"

"That is not any of your business Kagan, how much were you paid to stop me from interviewing Jason"

"I can not disclose that information-it is confidential, just as I am not allowed to disclose the ten years of intensive therapy that I gave you Mr. Mitchell Martinez; now, why don't you just go home, back to your lovely wife and children and let the professionals handle this case"

"It was your professionals that got the man into this murderous mind control in the first place Kagan"

"What, what do you mean now Mitchell"

"The reason that they hired you is to prevent me from writing the article that shows and tells how Uber Drove this dam man crazy-well, I am going to write everything about the circumstances Kagan-how Uber subjected Jason to those awful hours of working constantly cohering him to "Just Take One More Rider To Make A Even $100.00" You see Kagan, I drove for Uber and I know the tactics that they use-The Brain Subjective Mind Control Tactics that Uber Technicians place right on the Cell Phone that drives the drivers crazy" What a outside interview before Jason, the assumed uber driver, even came out to talk to me about his problem with Uber. That is the reason they hired me; they know that I knew what drove Jason crazy-It was Uber's Suggestive Subliminal Brain Washing Powers-that is what Uber stands for, it's Mission Statement-Uber's whole existence is based on pitting one group against the other for a profit-A Old Slave Trade Technique!

"Come back to Group Therapy, Mitchell; just think what you have already accomplished-A Five Star Driver for Uber, bonuses and accommodations; you will be losing a great deal of progress once you interview Jason"

"And how is that-how will I lose a digress once I have the interview of the Century"?

"Transference-you may very well, with your illness, transfer into Jason's madness of being a serial killer, how many more clients do we know of that were killed at the hands of this murderer"?

"Get out of here-you're the one that will transfer into a Serial Murderer, just like Hannibal, the Cannibal; what did you have for breakfast Kagan; a dead corpse from your laboratory at The VA"?

"You see, it has all ready began-those things that you are saying, why you need your medication-when was the last time that you took your medication Mitchell"

"I never took any of your medication-the only time I took some of that V A medication is when I got my legs severed off so those prosthetics could fit right into the socket-now, I refuse to go into the interviewing room with you-you're the one that is crazy, very sick individual"

"Very well-I will inform Mr. S., that I did talk to you and tried to convince you, not too interview the former Uber driver and we will notify The Rolling Stone Publishers that you have been in therapy for psychiatric reasons for the past ten years-that will discredit anything and everything that you write about Uber and the murderer"

"You know I am stronger than that-after going to war and having my legs blown too pieces what more can they do to me Kagan"

"You still have that one hand, that one arm-they will severe that one off if you are not careful"

"Threatening-I will have your license for that statement"

"Who you going to tell-who are you going to call, no one will listen to you-a double amputee that for the past twenty years lived at the Veterans Medical Center undergoing psychiatric therapy and surgery to correct a bosh Medical Surgical operation on your legs"

"They will"

"Who will Mitchell-are you hearing voices"

"No, but those cameras and video recorders can hear and see everything that you have told me and how you threathned me not to interview with Jason"

"Cameras, video taping-oh no, what have I done, what have I said-I will lose everything Mitchell, my license, my office my job-please do not report me; I will give them the Two Hundred and Fifty thousand Dollars back"

"That's what they gave you too stop me-wow" I told Kagan, the once psychiatrist that counseled me and brought up my confidence to go back into the world and make the best out of a bad situation. I called the bailiff or the sheriff to make me a copy of the outside conference I just had with Kagan and I will keep that copy in a safe place just in case I need it to protect my own personal integrity.

Cling, Clang, goes the electric doors leading to the prison block of Jason Dalton, The Uber-Murderer. Why was he labeling the Uber Murderer? It was because the person in the vehicle, bearing a Shot Gun, went around the city of Kalamazoo, shooting and killing innocent people while driving and working for Uber. The media label the man as an Uber-nator, a killer of people while working for Uber. That is how it goes in society of prolific, sensationalism and every journalist wants to be awarded the Pulitzer Prize in journalism. There he was the Uber-cide, the assumed murderer wearing an orange jump suit.

I walked into the one glass see through protective glass interview room and Jason, tried to get out of his chair but the guards restrain him.

"GROOVER, the UBER-GROOVER" said Jason; as a sudden glow came upon him as he looked at me and it was as if, I would not come too visit him, I would not be there for him; I would evade him and his needs to conveyed in me, for the whole world to read, what the hell happened in your mind that you killed, without any prejudice six innocent law abiding people?

"We only have SHORT TIME JASON, lets cut to the chase," I said.

"Thank you, for meeting with me GROOVER"

"Jason, what was in your head to have killed so many people-they were your people, they were people in your community-what happened"

"UBER Happened"

Stay Tuned for the next novel: UBERCIDE....Life of a UBER DRIVER....

The UBER-GROOVER, is a novel about the drivers of UBER, and this is just a synopsis of the Tales of the Lives of everyday driving for UBER. The facts are true and the characters names have been changed to protect the dedicated drivers whom, to this day, in the year of our Lord, 2017, are still a Slave for the UBER, Enterprize!

THE UBER-GROOVER; BIOGRAPHER, M J MANLEY.

Review Requested:

If you loved this book, would you please provide
a review at Amazon.com?